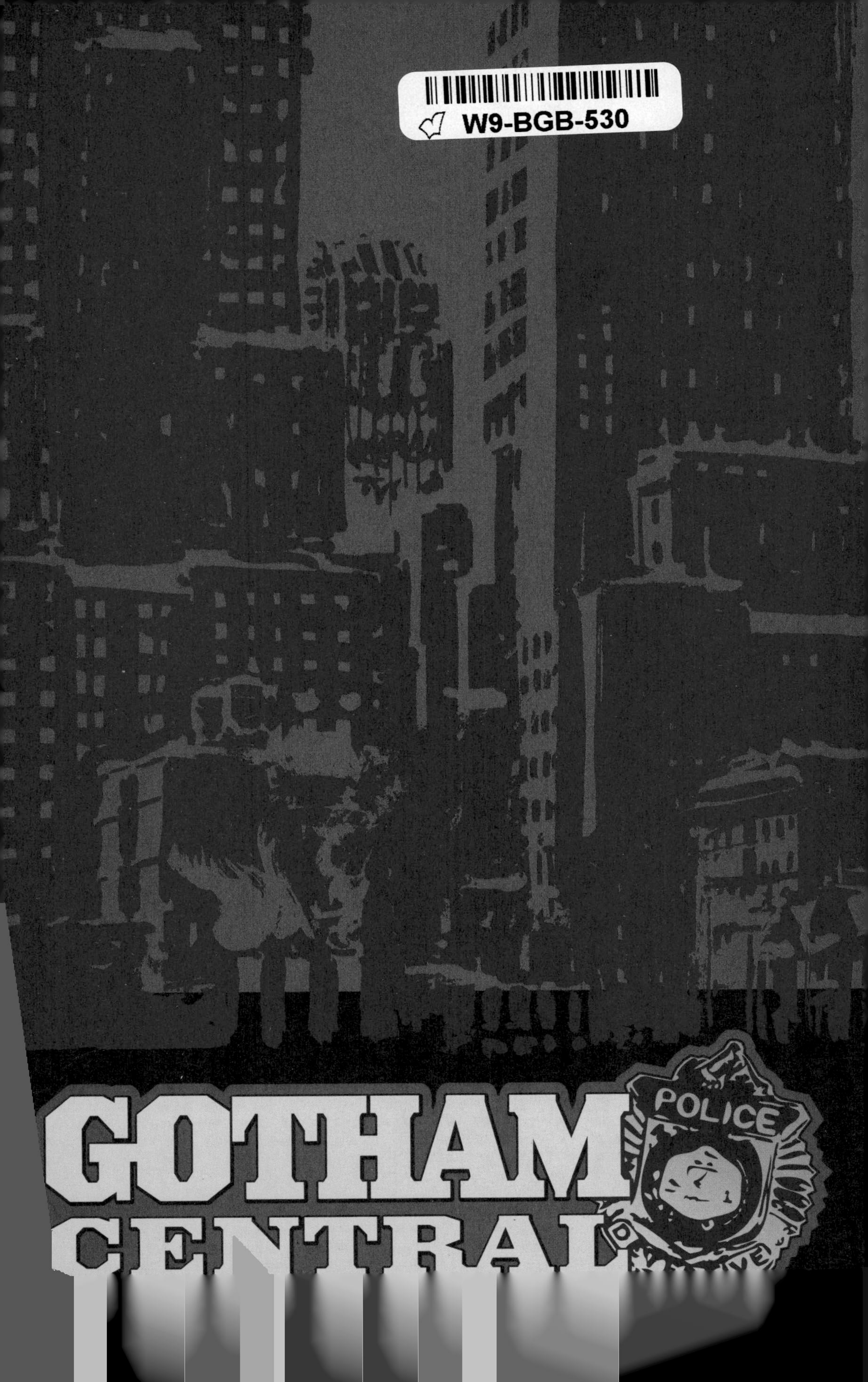
GOTHAM
CENTRAL
POLICE

Dan DiDio SENIOR VP-EXECUTIVE EDITOR • Matt Idelson EDITOR - ORIGINAL SERIES • Nachie Castro ASSOCIATE EDITO
ORIGINAL SERIES • Bob Joy EDITOR - COLLECTED EDITION • Robbin Brosterman SENIOR ART DIRECTOR • Paul Levitz PRESIDENT
PUBLISHER • Georg Brewer VP-DESIGN & DC DIRECT CREATIVE • Richard Bruning SENIOR VP-CREATIVE DIRECTOR • Patrick Cald
EXECUTIVE VP-FINANCE & OPERATIONS • Chris Caramalis VP-FINANCE • John Cunningham VP-MARKETING • Terri Cunningha
VP-MANAGING EDITOR • Stephanie Fierman SENIOR VP-SALES & MARKETING • Alison Gill VP-MANUFACTURING • Hank Kana
VP-GENERAL MANAGER, WILDSTORM • Lillian Laserson SENIOR VP & GENERAL COUNSEL • Jim Lee EDITORIAL DIRECTOR – WILDSTOR
Paula Lowitt SENIOR VP-BUSINESS & LEGAL AFFAIRS • David McKillips VP-ADVERTISING & CUSTOM PUBLISHING • John N
VP-BUSINESS DEVELOPMENT • Gregory Noveck SENIOR VP-CREATIVE AFFAIRS • Cheryl Rubin SENIOR VP-BRAND MANAGEME
Jeff Trojan VP-BRAND MANAGEMENT, DC DIRECT • Bob Wayne VP-SALES

GOTHAM CENTRAL: THE QUICK AND THE DEAD

COVER ILLUSTRATION BY Michael Lark • GOTHAM SKYLINE INKED BY Stefano Gaudiano

GOTHAM CENTRAL

THE QUICK AND THE DEAD

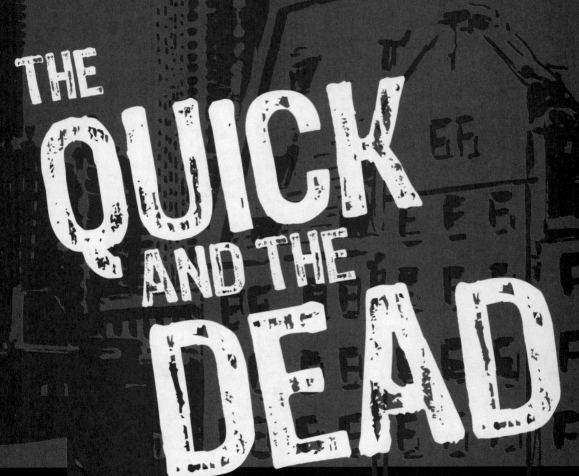

GREG RUCKA WRITER

MICHAEL LARK & STEFANO GAUDIANO
PENCILLERS

STEFANO GAUDIANO, KANO
& GARY AMARO INKERS

LEE LOUGHRIDGE COLORIST

CLEM ROBINS LETTERER

BATMAN CREATED BY **BOB KANE**

GOTHAM CITY POLICE DEPARTMENT,

MAJOR CRIMES UNIT

**CAPTAIN
MAGGIE SAWYER**
First shift commander;
formerly head of Metropolis
Special Crimes Unit.

**SGT. VINCENT
DEL ARRAZIO**
First shift
second-in-command;
partner of Joely Bartlett.

**DETECTIVE
ANDI KASINSKY**
Partner of Eric Cohen.

**DETECTIVE
JOSEPHINE "JOSIE
MAC" MacDONALD**
Has the distinction of being
the first MCU officer selected
after Jim Gordon's retirement.

LT. DAVID CORNWELL
Second shift commander.

SECOND SHIFT →

**SGT. JACKSON
"SARGE" DAVIES**
Second shift co-second-in-
command; partner of Crowe.

LT. RON PROBSON
Second shift co-second-in-
command.

**DETECTIVE
TREY HARTLEY**
Partner of Josh Azeveda.

**DETECTIVE
NATE PATTON**
Partner of Romy Chandler.

**POLICE
SUPPORT →**

**COMMISSIONER
MICHAEL AKINS**
Former commissioner for
Gateway City, replaced
James W. Gordon.

**DETECTIVE
CRISPUS ALLEN**
Partner of Renee Montoya.

**DETECTIVE
JOELY BARTLETT**
Partner of Vincent
Del Arrazio.

**DETECTIVE
TOMMY BURKE**
Partner of
Dagmar Procjnow.

**DETECTIVE
ERIC COHEN**
Partner of Andi Kasinsky.

**DETECTIVE 2ND GRADE
RENEE MONTOYA**
Partner of Crispus Allen.

**DETECTIVE
DAGMAR PROCJNOW**
Partner of Tommy Burke.

FIRST SHIFT
←

**DETECTIVE
JOSH AZEVEDA**
Partner of Trey Hartley.

**DETECTIVE
ROMY CHANDLER**
Partner of Nate Patton.

DETECTIVE CROWE
Partner of "Sarge" Davies.

**DETECTIVE
MARCUS DRIVER**
Last MCU officer to be select-
ed by former Commissioner
James W. Gordon.

JIM CORRIGAN
GCPD crime scene
investigator.

NORA FIELDS
City coroner.

JAMES W. GORDON
Former Gotham City police
commissioner, and 20-year
veteran of the force. Currently
teaches criminology at
Gotham University.

STACY
Receptionist; only person
permitted to operate the
Bat-Signal.

GOTHAM CENTRAL

CORRIGAN

PART ONE

GREG RUCKA
WRITER

MICHAEL LARK
PENCILLER

STEFANO GAUDIANO
INKER

SUNDAY WILL WORK, BUT IT HAS TO BE AFTER ELEVEN.

DORE AND I WERE THINKING WE'D COME OVER AFTER CHURCH, DARIA CAN *WOW* US WITH HER CULINARY SKILL.

SHE WILL, TOO. SHE DOES A *FRITTATA* LIKE NOBODY'S BUSINESS, TELL YOU THAT MUCH.

YOUR WOMAN CAN FRITTATA-TA-TA ALL SHE *LIKES*, BUT I'VE GOT *TWO* KIDS, AND THEY SPEAK *ONE* WORD AT SUNDAY BREAKFAST...

...AND THAT WORD IS *"WAFFLES."*

SHE DOES WAFFLES LIKE NOBODY'S BUSINESS, TOO.

YOU OR ME THIS TIME?

ALL YOURS, PARTNER.

DETECTIVE MONTOYA, YOU *STILL* TRYING TO *PAY* ME FOR YOUR FOOD?

I AM, GINNY.

GIRL, WE GOT *GANGS* SHOOTING THIS CITY TO *HELL* AND *BACK* RIGHT NOW!

I TOLD *YOU* AND I TOLD YOUR *PARTNER*, YOUR MONEY'S NO GOOD HERE.

SHE'S *SLOW*, GINNY, YOU HAVE TO *FORGIVE* HER.

I LEAVE *FORGIVENESS* TO THE ALMIGHTY, DETECTIVE ALLEN.

YOU *FEEL* THAT? IT'S LIKE WALKING INTO A *SPONGE.*

HALF PAST *MIDNIGHT,* THE HUMIDITY'S *STILL* A ZILLION PERCENT.

PLEASE TELL ME THE *AIR CONDITIONER* WORKS.

OKAY, THE AIR CONDITIONER WORKS.

SMART-ASS

AND SEXY, TOO.

HUNTING PARTY.

B.T.M.

CALL FOR BACKUP.

CENTRAL SIX-CHARLIE-TANGO, TEN THIRTY-ONE, EIGHT THOUSAND BLOCK OF HEWLIS, REQUEST BACKUP.

SIX-CHARLIE-TANGO STAND BY.

SIX-CHARLIE-TANGO, BE ADVISED, BACKUP EN ROUTE...

...E.T.A. *FIVE* MINUTES.

KRAKKRAKKRAK
KRAK KRAK

FIVE MINUTES.

YOU WANT TO *WAIT*?

THAT'S WHAT I THOUGHT.

THEY STARTED WITHOUT US.

HOW RUDE.

JESUS, CRIS, THIS KID'S *SIXTEEN* IF A DAY.

YOU RECOGNIZE THIS *TAG*? IT'S *NOT* BURNLEY TOWN MASSIVE.

KRAK KRAK
KRAK KRAK

CHAK CHAK CHAK
CHAK CHAK
CHAK

HNNN

MUH-MUH
FUHNNNN

MAN, CAN'T *SEE* HIM!

KEEP LOOKING! HE AROUND HERE SOMEWHERE!

POLICE! **FREEZE!**

LOSE THE GUNS, TOUGH GUY.

BIG FRONT, YOU **SOUND** LIKE A SMALL GIRL.

MY **PISTOL** MAKES UP FOR IT.

NOW *LOSE* THE GUNS, I WON'T SAY IT AGAIN.

SHE MEANS YOU, TOO.

ON THE *FLOOR*, BOTH OF YOU.

WE BEEN *HAD*, BUNK. SPIDER'S DONE *BOUGHT* HIMSELF SOME *POLICE*...

...THEY PROBABLY *WIPE* FOR HIM, TOO.

THE HELL ARE YOU TALKING ABOUT?

HEY, I KNOW MY *RIGHTS*, I DON'T TELL YOU *SQUAT*.

YEAH? THEN *SHUT UP*.

KRK

THERE'S *ONE* MORE.

FIVE-TO-ONE IT'S A *FREAK*.

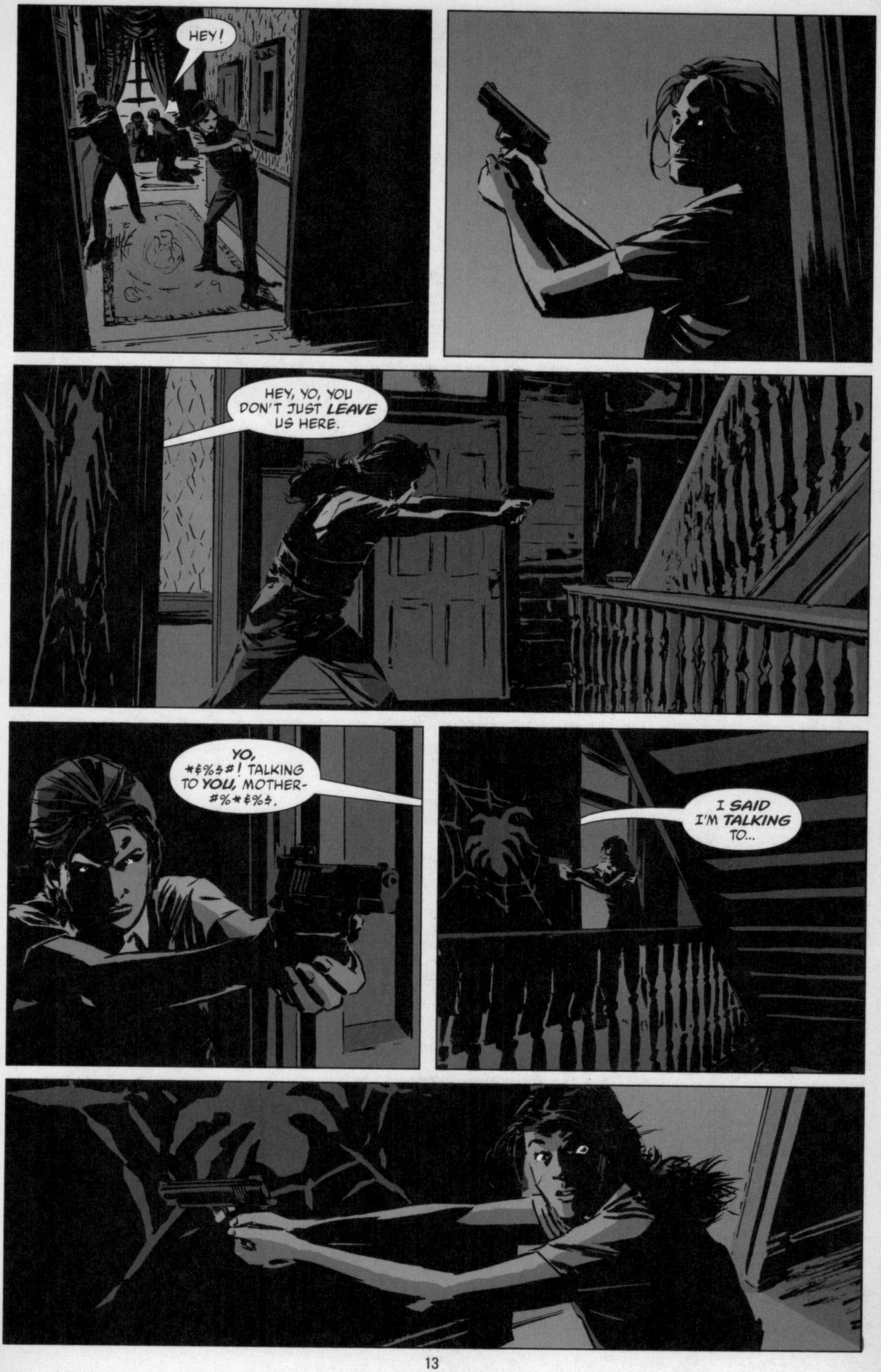
HEY!
HEY, YO, YOU DON'T JUST LEAVE US HERE.
YO, *$%$#! TALKING TO YOU, MOTHER-#%*$%$.
I SAID I'M TALKING TO...

CHAKACHAKA
CHAKACHAKA

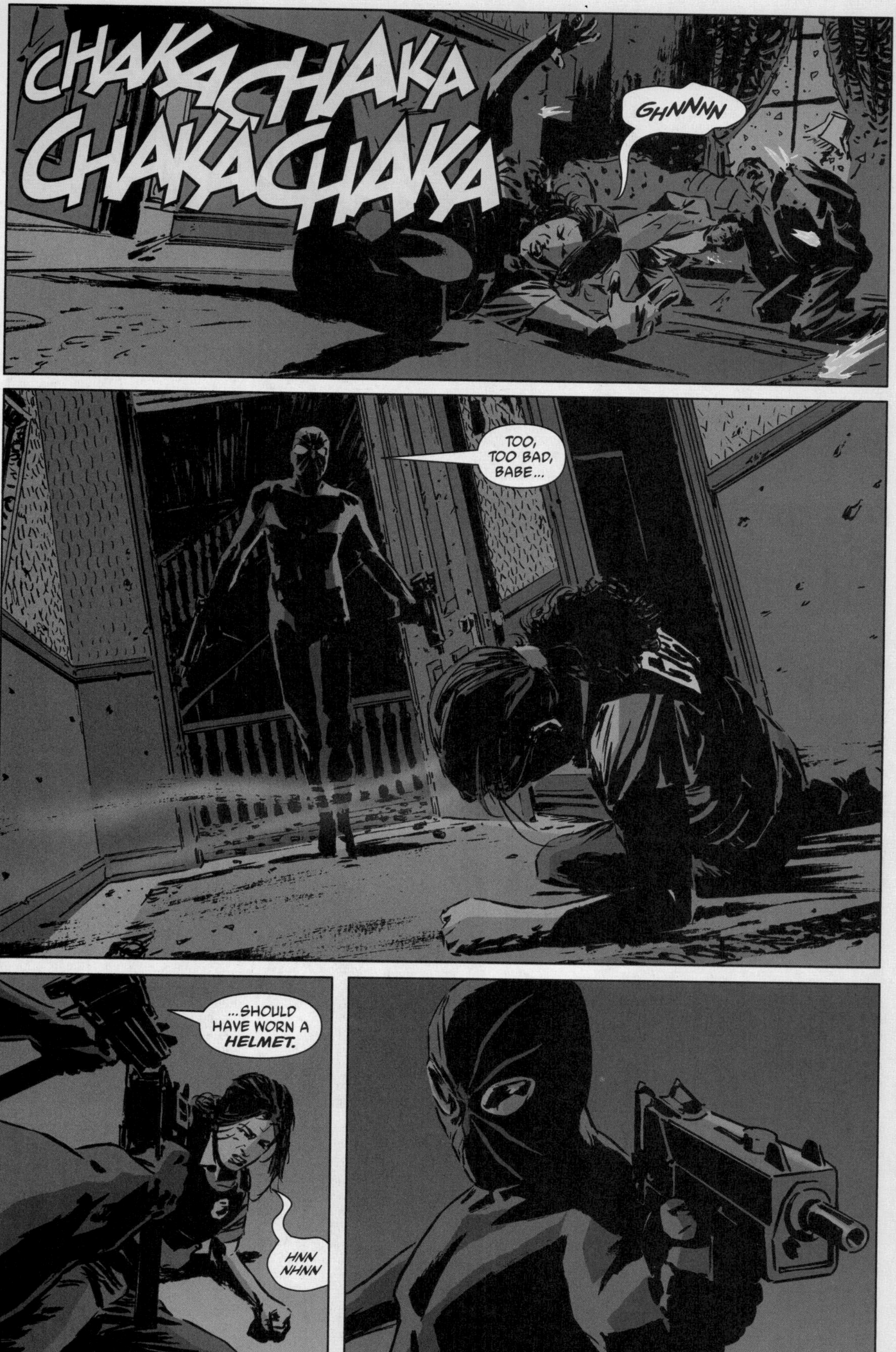
CHAKACHAKA
CHAKACHAKA
GHNNNN
TOO, TOO BAD, BABE...
...SHOULD HAVE WORN A HELMET.
HNN NHNN

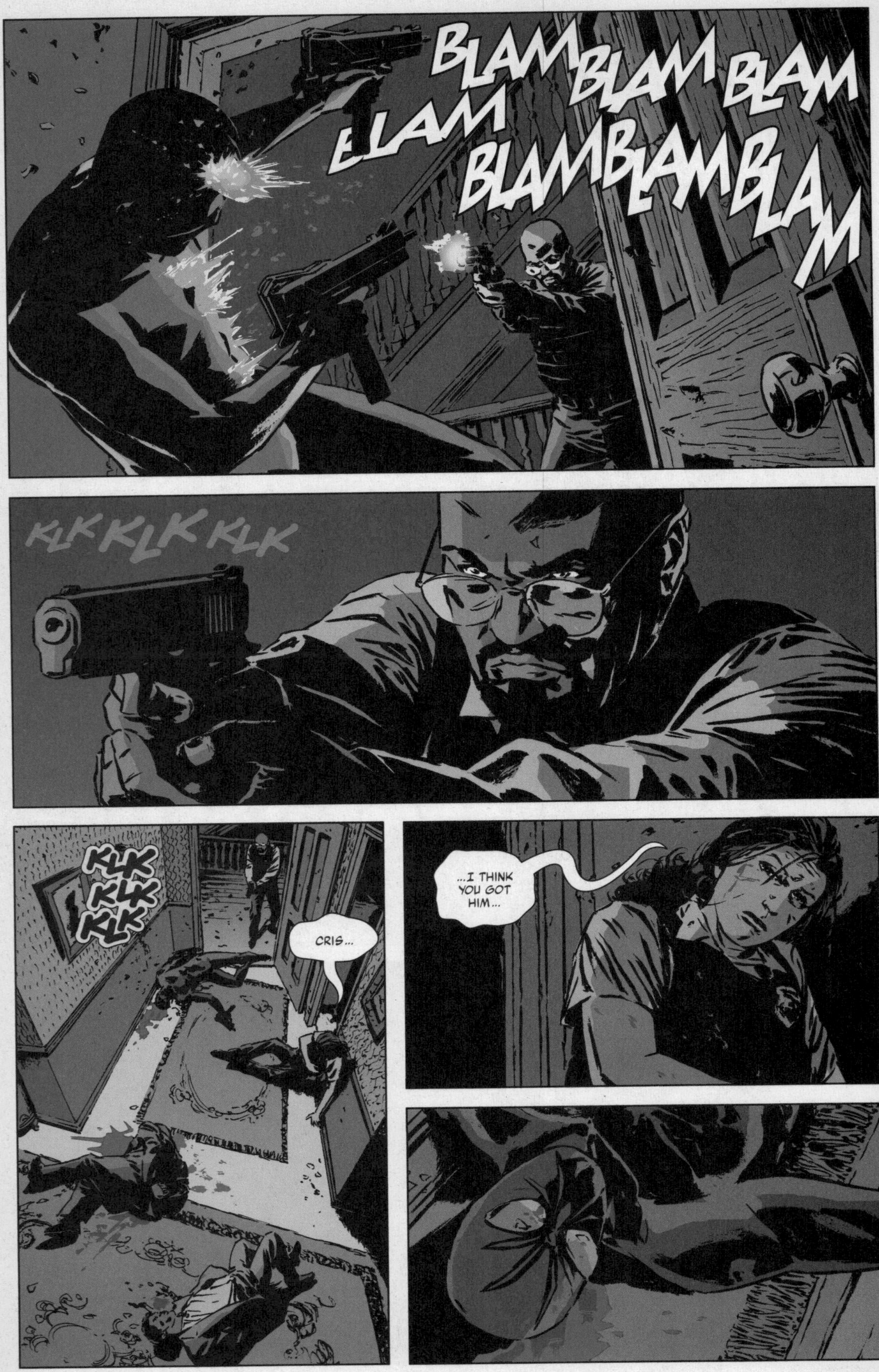
BLAM BLAM BLAM
BLAM
BLAM BLAM BLAM
KLK KLK KLK
KLK
KLK
KLK
CRIS...
...I THINK YOU GOT HIM...

HOLD
UP.

ESPERANZA.

GOT HERE
ABOUT FIVE
MINUTES AGO,
CAPTAIN.

DAMMIT.

DETECTIVE
ALLEN!

UP HERE,
CAPTAIN.

STOP
TALKING TO
ESPERANZA.

IF HE'S *NOT* SUPPOSED TO TALK TO ME, HOW AM I SUPPOSED TO *CLEAR* HIM FOR THE *SHOOT?*

YOU COULD GIVE HIM A COUPLE MINUTES TO COLLECT HIMSELF.

YOU KNOW THE *RULES,* MAGGIE. I HAVE TO TAKE THE *STATEMENT* AS SOON AS POSSIBLE.

YOU ALL RIGHT, CRIS?

MY STOMACH'S SETTLING.

HOW'S *RENEE?*

SHE'S AT THE *HOSPITAL.* TWO OF HER *RIBS* CRACKED, BUT OTHERWISE SHE'S FINE.

THANK GOD FOR THAT.

LET'S FINISH THIS UP, DETECTIVE.

RIGHT...I...WE'D *CUFFED* THE TWO IN THE *APARTMENT,* THEN HEARD SOMETHING IN THE *HALL.*

I WENT TO CIRCLE AROUND, AS I WAS COMING OUT I HEARD THE *SHOTS.* MY WEAPON WAS ALREADY *OUT.*

I CAME AROUND, SAW THE *FREAK.*

"BLACK SPIDER." REAL NAME WAS JOHNNY LAMONICA.

RIGHT, I SAW HIM *HERE,* HE WAS *SHOOTING* INTO THE *APARTMENT.*

HE'D ALREADY HIT DETECTIVE MONTOYA?

IT WAS... IT WAS ALL AT ONCE, HE'D HIT HER, SHE WAS FALLING, HE WAS *STILL* SHOOTING.

THAT MUST HAVE BEEN WHEN HE HIT THE *OTHER* TWO, THE ONES WE'D *ARRESTED.*

THAT'S WHAT I SAW.

HE WAS POINTING A GUN--ONE OF HIS GUNS--AT RENEE, HE LEVELED THE *OTHER* ONE AT ME...

I STARTED *SHOOTING.*

THAT'S IT, THAT'S ALL.

NOTHING YOU WANT TO ADD?

HE SAID THAT'S *ALL,* MANNY.

I'M GONNA NEED THE *STATEMENT* IN *WRITING.* HE CAN DO THAT WHEN HE GETS BACK TO CENTRAL.

YOU'LL HAVE IT.

MONTOYA'S AT GENERAL?

THEY TOOK HER TO ST. LUKE'S, ALONG WITH THE *OTHER* BANGER.

I'LL TALK TO HER *THERE,* THEN.

NEED YOUR *WEAPON,* DETECTIVE.

...RIGHT.

YOU'LL BE GETTING IT BACK, I'M SURE.

LET'S GET YOU BACK TO CENTRAL.

HUH?

YEAH... YEAH, LET'S DO THAT...

JUST FOR THE **STATEMENT**, CRIS, THEN YOU CAN GO HOME.

NO, I'M FINE, CAPTAIN, IT'S OKAY.

RENEE'S OKAY?

SHE'LL BE FINE.

SHE SAYS YOU SAVED HER LIFE.

FINISHED WITH THE *DOORWAY*, YOU WANT TO TAKE SOME SHOTS OUT THERE.

I SWEAR WE'RE GONNA BE HERE UNTIL *NOON*, CORRIGAN.

HEY, IT'S ALL GOOD, *FRANKIE*.

NOTHING LIKE A NICE BIG *GANG WAR* TO BOOST THE *SAVINGS ACCOUNT*...

...WE GET *O.T.*, AND THE *SKELS* KILL EACH OTHER OFF.

THAT'S *WIN-WIN* WHERE I'M SITTING...

...MONEY IN *POCKET*...

...NO, HER NAME IS MONTOYA, RENEE MONTOYA.

ARE YOU FAMILY?

I'M HER *PARTNER.*

THEN I *NEED* TO SEE A *BADGE.*

NO, I'M *NOT* A COP, I'M HER...WE *LIVE* TOGETHER.

SHE'S YOUR GIRLFRIEND.

SHE'S MY *PARTNER.*

WHATEVER, YOU'RE GOING TO HAVE TO *WAIT* HERE, LIKE EVERYONE ELSE.

CHEF HERNANDEZ.

OH, CHRIST.

I GUESS I MADE AN *IMPRESSION.*

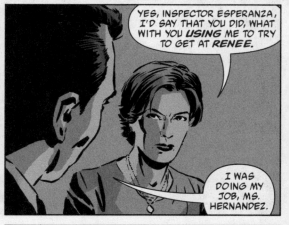

YES, INSPECTOR ESPERANZA, I'D SAY THAT YOU DID, WHAT WITH YOU *USING* ME TO TRY TO GET AT *RENEE.*

I WAS DOING MY JOB, MS. HERNANDEZ.

WON'T LET YOU BACK TO SEE HER?

I'M NOT *FAMILY* ENOUGH.

NOT LIKE *ANY* OF HER FAMILY IS HERE, OF COURSE.

WELL, COME ON.

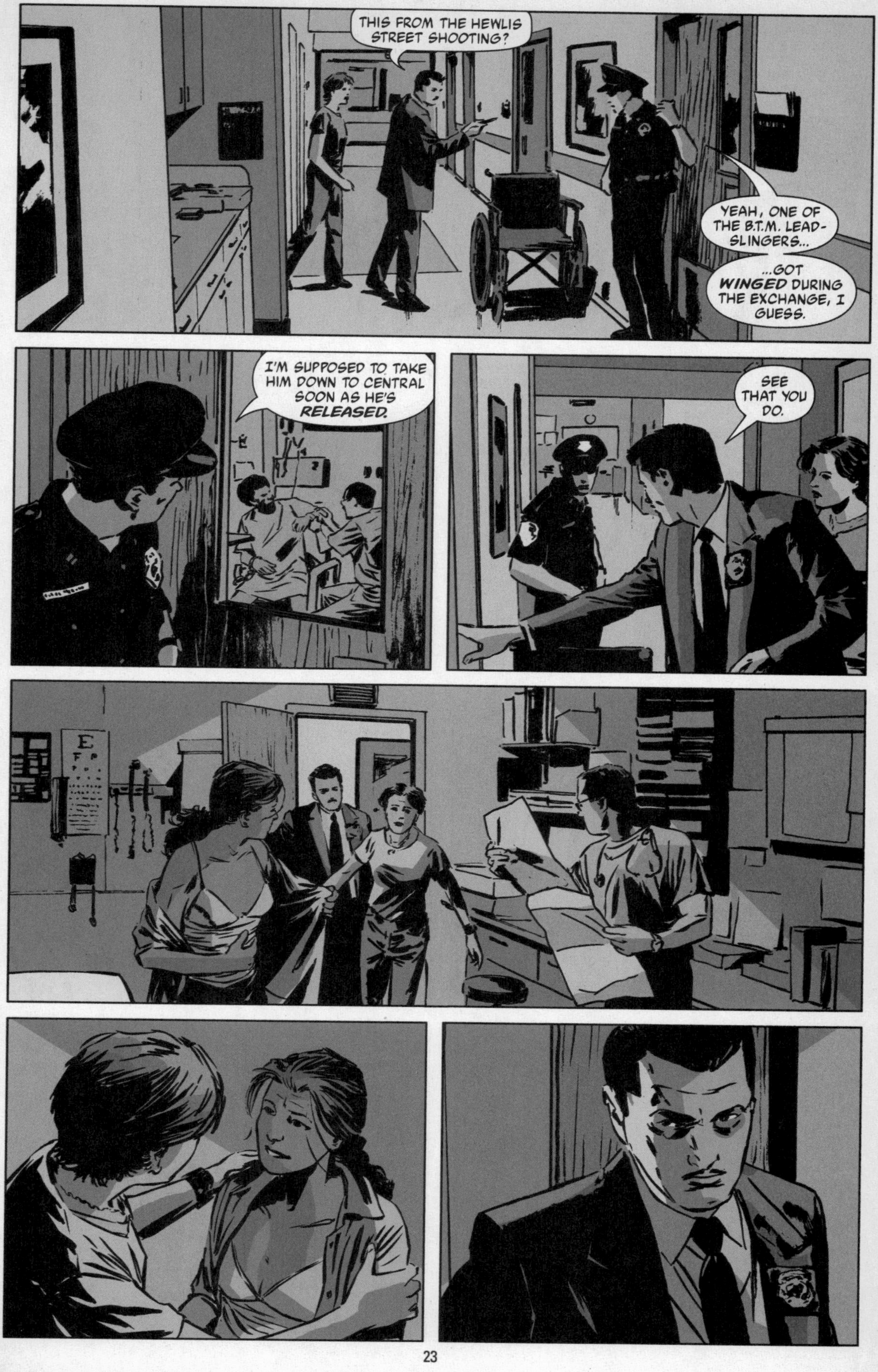
THIS FROM THE HEWLIS STREET SHOOTING?
YEAH, ONE OF THE B.T.M. LEAD-SLINGERS...
...GOT WINGED DURING THE EXCHANGE, I GUESS.
I'M SUPPOSED TO TAKE HIM DOWN TO CENTRAL SOON AS HE'S RELEASED.
SEE THAT YOU DO.
E

HE WAS ABOUT TO PULL THE TRIGGER ON ME, INSPECTOR, SWEAR TO GOD THE *NEXT* BURST WAS COMING FOR MY *HEAD.*

CRIS HADN'T LIT HIM UP, I'D BE DEAD RIGHT NOW.

I DON'T DOUBT IT.

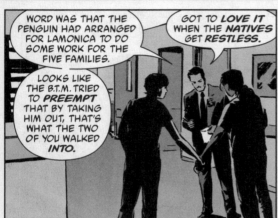

WORD WAS THAT THE PENGUIN HAD ARRANGED FOR LAMONICA TO DO SOME WORK FOR THE FIVE FAMILIES.

LOOKS LIKE THE B.T.M. TRIED TO *PREEMPT* THAT BY TAKING HIM OUT, THAT'S WHAT THE TWO OF YOU WALKED *INTO.*

GOT TO *LOVE IT* WHEN THE *NATIVES* GET *RESTLESS.*

HOW LONG IS THIS GOING TO TAKE?

WE'LL HAVE *DISPOSITION* ON THE *SHOOT* TOMORROW, I EXPECT.

IT WAS *RIGHTEOUS,* INSPECTOR.

HOPE-FULLY THAT'S HOW IT'LL CHECK OUT.

IT *WAS* A *CLEAN* SHOOT.

WHAT DO YOU WANT ME TO SAY, DETECTIVE? EVEN *IF* I THINK THAT, I CAN'T SAY IT, NOT YET.

ASK ME AGAIN *TOMORROW.*

ALL RIGHT, SIT HERE AND BE QUIET.

WHERE'M I GONNA GO, FOOL? YOU GOT ME *CUFFED* HERE!

TAKE IT EASY, GARY. WE'LL GET THIS ALL SORTED SOON ENOUGH.

DAMN, I GOT *SHOT*, MAN! I SHOULD BE *HOME* IN *BED*.

INSPECTOR ESPERANZA?

YOUR *SUSPECT* IS HERE.

HE BROUGHT THAT *ATTORNEY*, FINN RICKERT.

JESUS.

FINN RICKERT?

AMBULANCE CHASER.

PUT THEM IN INTERVIEW ONE, PLEASE.

YES, SIR.

YOU ALREADY SIGNED IT.

NO REASON *NOT* TO.

ALL RIGHT.

CAPTAIN SAWYER'S PUT YOU ON ADMIN UNTIL THIS IS *RESOLVED.*

BETWEEN YOU AND ME, DETECTIVE, YOU'VE GOT NOTHING TO WORRY ABOUT.

JUST PAPERWORK FROM HERE ON OUT.

YEAH, SHE TOLD ME.

THAT'S HIM!

THAT'S THE ONE WHO *SHOT* ME, MAN, AND I WAS *HANDCUFFED* AND ALL THAT!

YOU'RE *SURE* ABOUT THAT, GARY?

THE HELL ARE YOU TALKING ABOUT?

I'M TALKING ABOUT *YOU!*

TRYING TO *KILL* A *BROTHER* WHEN HE'S *HAND-CUFFED!*

THAT'S ENOUGH...

...YOU GOT SOMETHING TO SAY, SAY IT IN THE BOX.

EASY, THERE, INSPECTOR...

...I LIKE TO KEEP MY *LAW-SUITS* AGAINST THE *DEPARTMENT* COMING *ONE* AT A TIME...

...INSTEAD OF ALL AT *ONCE.*

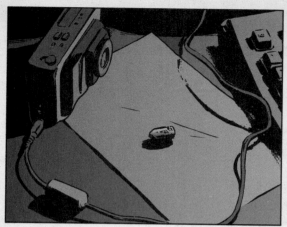

This UNIQUE and ONE OF A KIND item is available for a limited time only! The BULLET that KILLED the infamous Johnny LaMonica, AKA The Black Spider, notorious assassin employed by such villains as Black Mask, the Penguin, and others!

A must for any collection of Gotham crime_

Current bid:

Time left:

US $1.000

Place Bid >

6 days 23 hours
7 day listing
Ends Jun

COME TO
PAPA.

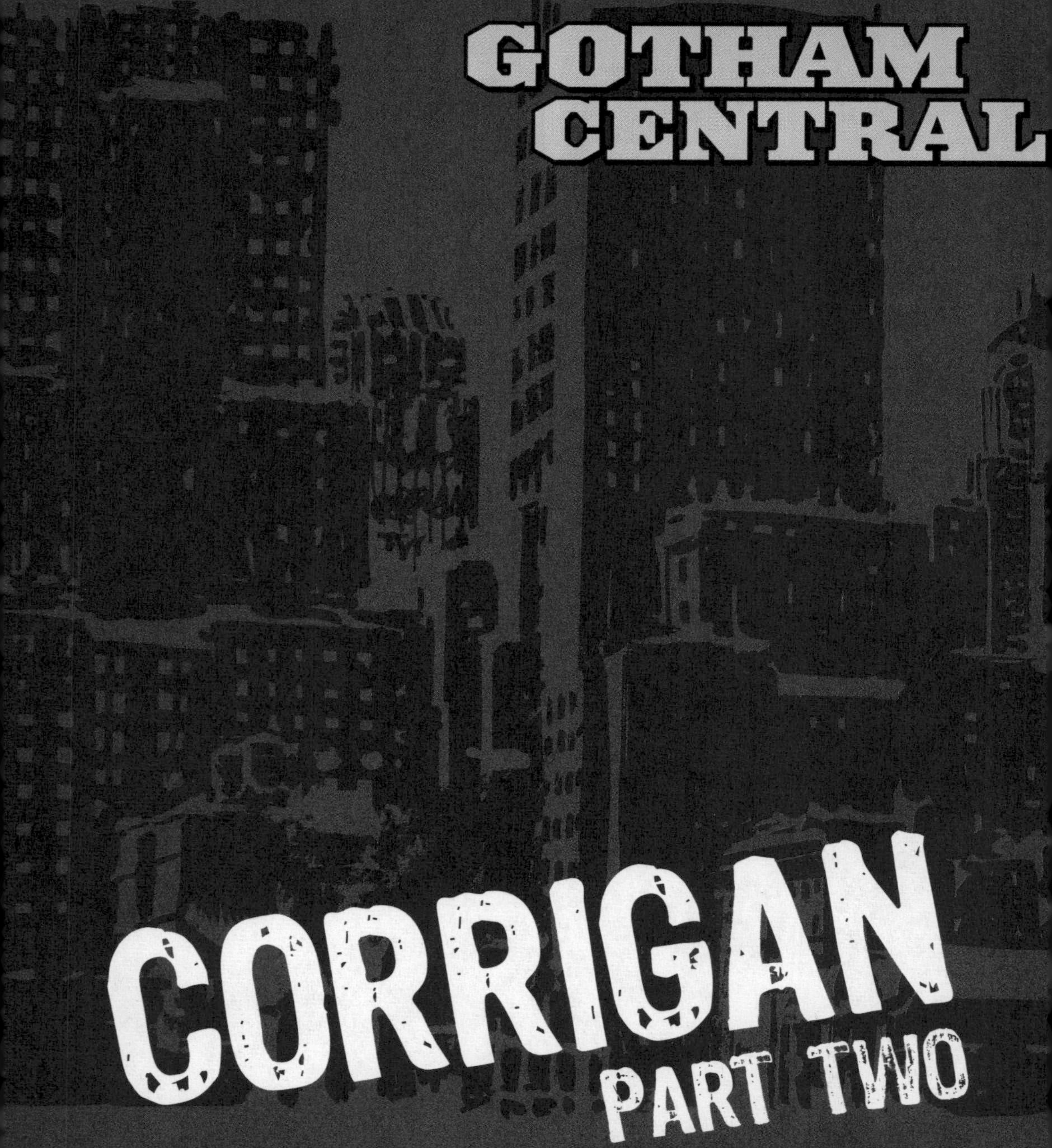

GOTHAM CENTRAL

CORRIGAN
PART TWO

GREG RUCKA
WRITER

MICHAEL LARK
PENCILLER

STEFANO GAUDIANO
INKER

HEY, LET ME *HELP.*

UH, *NO,* DORE, YOU JUST *SIT* TIGHT.

WOULDN'T BE MUCH OF AN INVITATION TO *BRUNCH* IF WE LET YOU DO THE *DISHES.*

IT'S THE *DISTRIBUTION* OF *LABOR* AROUND HERE.

YEAH, SHE *COOKS,* I DO THE DISHES.

CRIS, GIVE ME A *HAND?*

WHAT, I DON'T *QUALIFY* AS A *GUEST?*

NO.

DEE, YOU SIT, TOO, YOU DID *YOUR* PART.

DON'T CARRY TOO MUCH.

MY *RIBS* ARE *FINE.*

YOUR RIBS ARE *CRACKED,* MY LOVE.

JAKE, MAL, MAKE YOURSELVES *USEFUL.*

HELP CLEAR THE TABLE.

YOU'VE GOT *GOOD* KIDS.

MOST OF THE TIME.

DO THE *BOYS* KNOW WHAT HAPPENED? ABOUT THE *SHOOTING?*

CRIS AND I TALKED ABOUT IT, DECIDED IT'D BE *BEST* TO TELL THEM.

WITH THE *LAWSUIT* AND *EVERYTHING,* WE DIDN'T WANT THEM TO HEAR ABOUT IT IN THE *NEWS.*

JAKE UNDERSTANDS IT *BETTER,* HE'S ALMOST *SEVENTEEN.* BUT MALCOLM, HE'S FOURTEEN, HE HAD TROUBLE WITH IT.

WE'VE ALWAYS *RAISED* THE BOYS TELLING THEM *VIOLENCE* ISN'T A *SOLUTION.*

CRIS FINALLY TOLD HIM THAT THERE WASN'T *ANY* OTHER *CHOICE.*

HE TOLD HIM THAT LAMONICA WAS ABOUT TO *MURDER* HIS PARTNER.

HE WAS TRYING TO *SAVE* RENEE'S *LIFE.*

HE *DID.*

THANKS, GUYS.

THERE'S A **VIDEO GAME** CONSOLE HOOKED UP TO THE TV, IF YOU WANT TO **SAVE** THE **EARTH** FROM AN ALIEN **INVASION** OR SOMETHING.

SICK!

CAN WE, DAD?

YOU MAY.

QUIETLY.

VIDEO GAMES?

THEY'RE DEE'S, I SWEAR.

SURE.

I TALKED TO **ESPERANZA** ON FRIDAY.

HE SAYS FINN RICKERT'S ALL SET TO **DEPOSE** YOU THIS WEEK.

HE SHOULDN'T HAVE TOLD YOU THAT.

IT'S **ALL** BULL#‡*, CRIS. THERE'S NO WAY IN **HELL** YOU COULD HAVE EVEN **HIT** THAT PUNK, WHAT'S HIS NAME?

GARY WATSON.

THE **ANGLE** WAS **TOTALLY** WRONG. IT HAS TO HAVE BEEN ONE OF LAMONICA'S **ROUNDS** THAT **WINGED** HIM.

YEAH.

THAT'S WHAT **I** KEEP SAYING, TOO.

PROBLEM IS, IT'S NOT WHAT EITHER GARY WATSON OR FINN RICKERT IS *CLAIMING.*

AND THERE'S *NO* EVIDENCE TO PROVE THEM *WRONG* AND ME *RIGHT.*

WHAT, C.S.U. DIDN'T *MATCH* ALL THE *ROUNDS?*

C.S.U., RENEE.

THESE GUYS LIFT A *CLEAN* PRINT, WE'RE LUCKY. YOU HONESTLY *SURPRISED* THAT THEY MISSED A COUPLE OF *BULLETS?*

HERE, USE THIS.

THANKS.

WHO WAS THE *LEAD* TECH?

CORRIGAN.

JESUS.

THERE'S YOUR PROBLEM.

TELL ME ABOUT IT.

BUT WHILE *YOU* AND ME AND MAYBE *HALF* THE M.C.U. KNOW HE'S ROTTEN...

...AIN'T *NOBODY* GOT *PROOF* THAT IT'S *SO.*

HEY, JO, GOT A MINUTE?

YOU GOTTA MAKE IT FAST, RENEE, MARCUS AND I HAVE TO *SERVE* A *WARRANT* ON THE RIDDLER THING.

YOU MAKING AN *ARREST*?

NAH, JUST A *SEARCH.* WHAT'S UP?

YOU KNOW CORRIGAN IN C.S.U., RIGHT?

JIMMY? I *KNOW* HIM, YEAH.

IT'S NOT LIKE WE'RE BUNKIES OR ANYTHING.

OKAY.

BECAUSE I HEARD YOU WERE *BANGING* THE *GUY.*

WHO THE *HELL* TOLD YOU *THAT*? DID MARCUS TELL YOU THAT?

NO, IT WASN'T DRIVER.

THEN *WHERE* THE *HELL* DO YOU GET OFF ASKING ME A QUESTION LIKE THAT?

IT'S JUST SOMETHING I HEARD, THAT'S ALL.

SO IT'S *CURIOSITY?* THAT'S IT?

SORRY TO *DISAPPOINT* YOU RENEE, BUT I *DON'T* PLAY FOR *YOUR* TEAM.

SOMEHOW I *MANAGE* TO SLEEP THROUGH THE NIGHT *ANYWAY.*

WHY'RE YOU ASKING ABOUT *CORRIGAN?*

BECAUSE I THINK THE *ROTTEN* SON OF A BITCH IS RESPONSIBLE FOR DROPPING MY *PARTNER* IN THE *JACKPOT.*

AND IF YOU *WERE* SLEEPING WITH HIM, MAYBE YOU'D *KNOW* SOMETHING ABOUT THAT.

&#$* YOU.

YOU WANT TO *ACCUSE* ME OF SOMETHING, MONTOYA, YA DO IT IN THE *BOX.*

OTHERWISE, KEEP THE *HELL* OUT OF MY *FACE.*

DETECTIVE MONTOYA.

SOMEONE PISSED IN DETECTIVE MACDONALD'S CORNFLAKES, IT SEEMS.

WHAT DO YOU *WANT,* ESPERANZA?

JUST SAYING HELLO.

WELL, *THAT* AND WONDERING IF IT WAS *YOU* WHO SET OFF MAC.

SHE TOOK *UMBRAGE* AT AN *INQUIRY* I MADE.

UMBRAGE. THAT'S A *GREAT* WORD, *UMBRAGE.*

AND WHAT CAUSED HER TO... *UMBER?*

I'D HEARD SHE AND CORRIGAN HAD A *THING.* WANTED TO SEE IF IT WAS *TRUE.*

IT *ISN'T.*

HELL, *I* COULD HAVE TOLD YOU *THAT,* MONTOYA. HE'S GOT A PIECE OVER AT *FINNIGAN'S.* YOU KNOW FINNIGAN'S, RIGHT, DETECTIVE?

OVER BY THE WESTERN. IT'S A *COP* BAR, IF WE *DEFINE* "COP" TO MEAN THAT *MAJORITY* OF THE G.C.P.D. ...

...WHO THINK CARRYING A *BADGE* IS AN *EXCUSE* TO LINE THEIR OWN *POCKETS...*

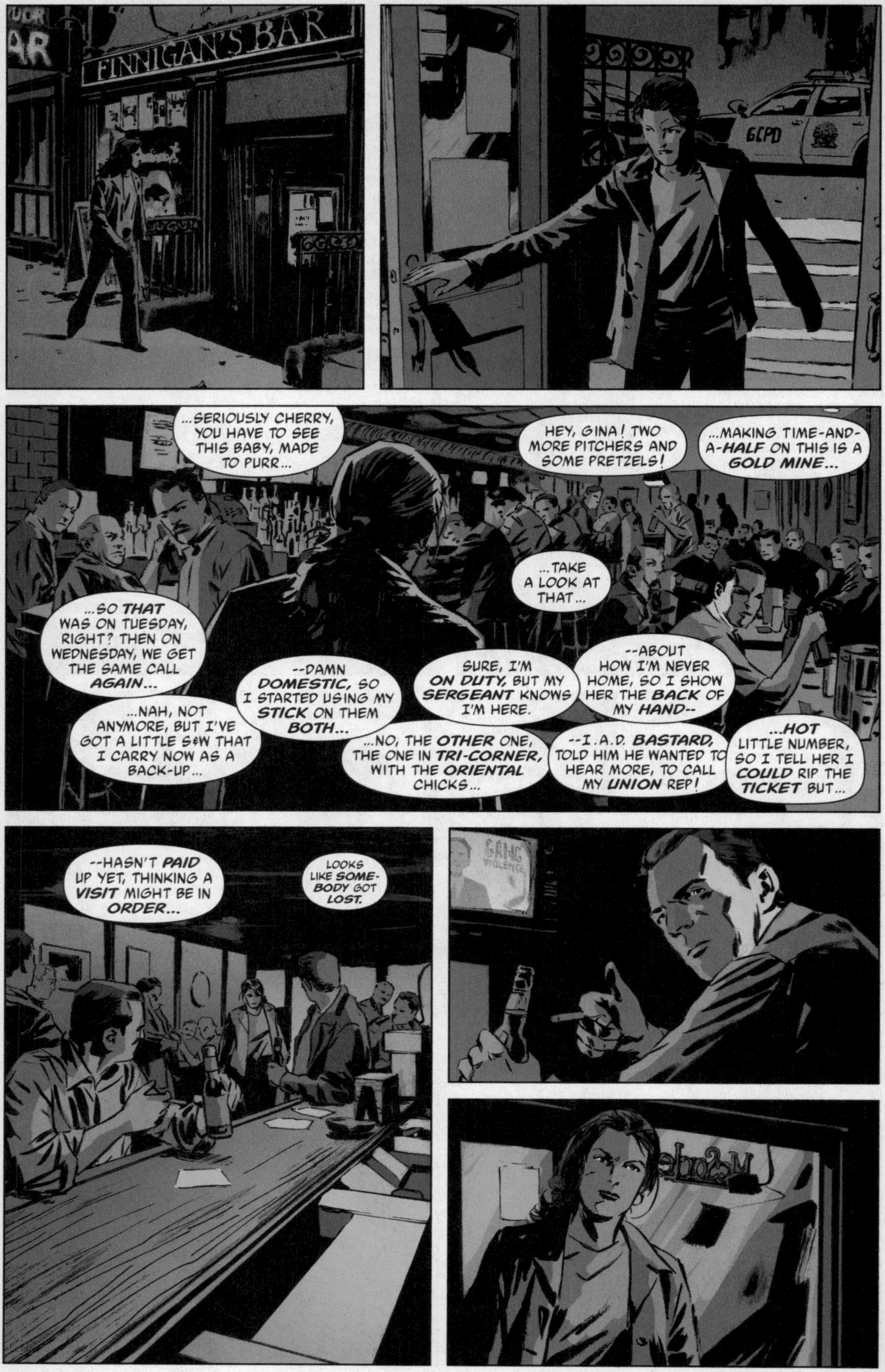
FINNIGAN'S BAR
GCPD
...SERIOUSLY CHERRY, YOU HAVE TO SEE THIS BABY, MADE TO PURR...
HEY, GINA! TWO MORE PITCHERS AND SOME PRETZELS!
...MAKING TIME-AND-A-HALF ON THIS IS A GOLD MINE...
...TAKE A LOOK AT THAT...
...SO THAT WAS ON TUESDAY, RIGHT? THEN ON WEDNESDAY, WE GET THE SAME CALL AGAIN...
...NAH, NOT ANYMORE, BUT I'VE GOT A LITTLE S&W THAT I CARRY NOW AS A BACK-UP...
--DAMN DOMESTIC, SO I STARTED USING MY STICK ON THEM BOTH...
SURE, I'M ON DUTY, BUT MY SERGEANT KNOWS I'M HERE.
...NO, THE OTHER ONE, THE ONE IN TRI-CORNER, WITH THE ORIENTAL CHICKS...
--ABOUT HOW I'M NEVER HOME, SO I SHOW HER THE BACK OF MY HAND--
--I.A.D. BASTARD, TOLD HIM HE WANTED TO HEAR MORE, TO CALL MY UNION REP!
...HOT LITTLE NUMBER, SO I TELL HER I COULD RIP THE TICKET BUT...
--HASN'T PAID UP YET, THINKING A VISIT MIGHT BE IN ORDER...
LOOKS LIKE SOMEBODY GOT LOST.
GANG VIOLENCE

M.C.U. DYKE.

CORRIGAN.

DETECTIVE MONTOYA.

YOU GET *LOST* OR SOME-THING?

I THOUGHT YOU M.C.U. TYPES WERE TOO *GOOD* TO *DRINK* WITH THE *WORKING CLASS.*

I'VE GOT SOME *QUESTIONS* FOR YOU ABOUT THE LAMONICA CRIME SCENE.

YOU CAN *READ MY REPORT.*

YOUR REPORT HAS SOME *HOLES* IN IT.

BULLET- SIZED ONES.

OH, WOW, THAT'S *CLEVER.* *BULLET-*SIZED ONES.

THERE ARE *ROUNDS* UNACCOUNTED FOR.

YOUR *REPORT* SAYS YOU RECOVERED *THIRTY-THREE* FROM THE SCENE.

BUT *BALLISTICS* ONLY HAS *THIRTY-TWO* OF THEM.

I *MISCOUNTED.*

RIGHT.

SO I GUESS *THAT* MEANS YOU'RE NOT ONLY *CROOKED,* YOU'RE *STUPID,* AS WELL.

I'D *BE* CAREFUL WHAT YOU'RE *SAYING,* DETECTIVE.

WHAT WITH YOU HAVING *CRACKED* RIBS AND *NO* BACKUP.

YOU WANT TO TAKE THIS *OUTSIDE,* JIMMY?

I'D BE *GLAD* TO TAKE THIS *OUTSIDE.*

YOU'RE *WEARING* YOUR PIECE, YOU NEED TO DITCH IT, DYKE.

I DON'T WANT YOU *SHOOTING* ME WHEN YOU *LOSE.*

CAN I SHOOT YOU WHEN I *WIN?*

HOLD THESE.

SEE HOW *ARROGANT* YOU ARE WITH *BROKEN* TEETH!

HNNFFF.

NGH.

AAAAHHHH!

UNNHHH

HOW'RE THOSE *RIBS*--

--YOU *STUCK* UP--

--SELF-RIGHTEOUS--

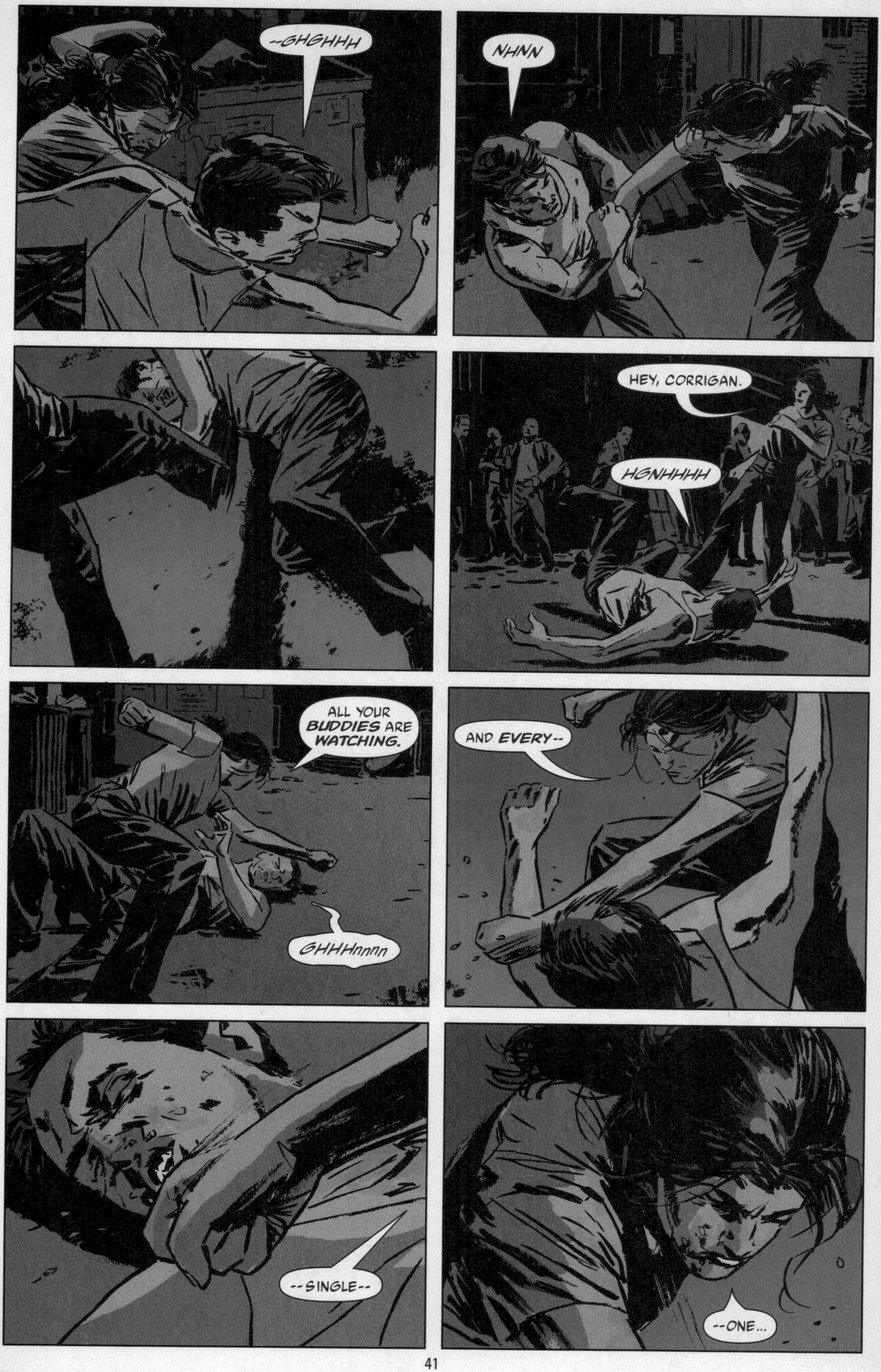
--GHGHHH
NHNN
HEY, CORRIGAN.
HGNHHHH
ALL YOUR BUDDIES ARE WATCHING.
GHHHnnnn
AND EVERY--
--SINGLE--
--ONE...

...JUST SAW *ME* HAND YOU YOUR *ASS.*

NOW, YOU GONNA COME *CLEAN,* OR AM I GONNA *BEAT* YOU SOME *MORE?*

GIVE IT SOME *THOUGHT,* JIMMY...

...BECAUSE I CAN DO THIS *ALL NIGHT...*

HE GIVE IT UP?

YOU **FOLLOW** ME?

DID HE GIVE IT **UP**, DETECTIVE?

HOW MUCH DID YOU **SEE**?

ENOUGH.

HE SOLD IT TO SOME **COLLECTOR** OUT IN THE 'BURBS FOR ALMOST **TEN** GRAND.

NAME OF **JENNIFER GORDON-HEWITT**.

THEN I'LL VISIT MS. HEWITT IN THE **MORNING**.

LIKE HELL.

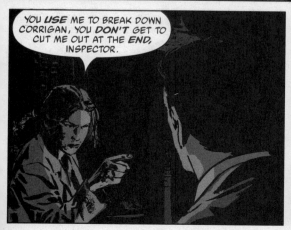

YOU **USE** ME TO BREAK DOWN CORRIGAN, YOU **DON'T** GET TO CUT ME OUT AT THE **END**, INSPECTOR.

I'LL MEET YOU AT **CENTRAL** IN THE **MORNING**...

...**WE** CAN TALK TO MS. HEWITT **TOGETHER**.

RENEE?

IT'S **OKAY.** GO BACK TO SLEEP, DEE.

DIDN'T MEAN TO **WAKE** YOU.

DID YOU GET INTO A **FIGHT?**

IT'S **NOTHING.** GO BACK TO SLEEP.

IT'S **NOT** NOTHING.

LET ME SEE.

OH, RENEE... YOU SHOULD SEE THE *OTHER* GUY.

IT'S *NOT* FUNNY!

I KNOW.

I DON'T *LIKE* THIS, I DON'T LIKE *YOU* LIKE THIS!

WOULD YOU *RATHER* I LIED?

NO, OF COURSE *NOT!*

I *KNOW* IT'S... IT'S A *VIOLENT* CITY...

...IT'S A VIOLENT *JOB,* EVEN...

...IT'S JUST...SOME-TIMES...

...SOMETIMES I THINK YOU *LIKE* THAT IT'S *VIOLENT...*

I DID WHAT I HAD TO *DO.*

I *GOT* WHAT I WAS *AFTER.*

LET ME DO THE TALKING.

YOU TRUST ME TO *BEAT* CORRIGAN, BUT NOT TO OPEN MY *MOUTH?*

EACH TO THEIR *ABILITES.*

WHAT'S *THAT* SUPPOSED TO MEAN?

YOU'RE A *DETECTIVE,* YOU FIGURE IT OUT.

I DON'T LIKE BEING *USED.*

I DIDN'T *MAKE* YOU DO *ANYTHING* YOU DIDN'T *WANT* TO, RENEE.

DONG DONG DONG

INSPECTOR MANUEL ESPERANZA, G.C.P.D., THIS IS DETECTIVE MONTOYA.

WERE LOOKING FOR JENNIFER GORDON-HEWITT.

OH, DEAR...

...THIS IS ABOUT THE *SCALPELS*, ISN'T IT?

I BOUGHT THEM IN *GOOD FAITH*, I WAS *ASSURED* THAT HE'D *NEVER* ACTUALLY GOTTEN AROUND TO *USING* THEM.

IMAGINE MY *SURPRISE* WHEN I *REALIZED* THERE WAS *DRIED BLOOD* ON THE *HANDLES*, I MEAN, I NEVER!

OH, DEAR. OH, DEAR OH, DEAR OH, DEAR ME.

SCALPELS?

PERHAPS YOU'D BETTER COME IN.

PERHAPS WE'D *BETTER*.

SCALPELS?

FOR MY *ZSASZ* SECTION, YES. I'VE *SEVERAL* PIECES DETAILING HIS *CAREER* IN MY *COLLECTION*, ACTUALLY.

YOUR *COLLECTION* OF...?

CRIME MEMORABILIA. IT'S MY *PASSION*, ESPECIALLY THE ITEMS AND OBJECTS OF GOTHAM'S MORE *NEFARIOUS* CRIMINALS.

THAT'S WHY YOU'RE *HERE*, I'M SURE. TO *VIEW* MY *COLLECTION*.

OF COURSE.

THOUGHT SO.

I KEEP THE *MAJORITY* IN HERE...

...BUT THERE'S *MUCH* MORE IN *STORAGE*, TOO.

IT WAS MY *LATE* HUSBAND WHO *STARTED* THE COLLECTION, OF COURSE. HE SAW THE BATMAN ONCE, FIGHTING THAT *CROCODILE* FELLOW.

AS *HE* TOLD IT--GOD REST HIS SOUL--BATMAN GAVE THAT PERPETRATOR A *MIGHTY* WALLOP, AND JUST LIKE *THAT*, ONE OF THOSE CROCODILE *TEETH* FLEW OUT OF HIS MOUTH.

LANDED RIGHT IN BARTHOLOMEW'S *LAP*, IT DID...

...THAT'S WHAT *STARTED* IT, OF COURSE. HE BROUGHT IT *HOME* AND *CLEANED* IT UP.

IT'S STILL *AROUND* HERE, SOMEWHERE, I THINK I COULD *DIG* IT OUT FOR YOU, IF YOU--

ACTUALLY, WE'RE LOOKING FOR A *BULLET* YOU PURCHASED *RECENTLY*.

WELL, DEAR... I'VE PURCHASED A *LOT* OF BULLETS, RECENTLY.

THIS *GANG WAR'S* BEEN A *BONANZA*, I'VE HAD TO SELL SOME *STOCK* JUST TO--

THIS IS FROM THE *BLACK SPIDER* KILLING.

SPENT A *PRETTY* PENNY ON *THAT.*

WELL, WE'LL BE *TAKING* IT WITH US.

NO, NO, DEAR, I *DON'T* THINK YOU *WILL*, NOT WITHOUT A *WARRANT* OF SOME SORT.

IT'S *MINE* FROM A *LEGAL* AND *LEGITIMATE* TRANSACTION.

IT'S *EVIDENCE* OF A *CRIME*--

OF COURSE IT IS, THAT'S WHY I BOUGHT IT.

--BUT *NOT* THE CRIME YOU *THINK.*

THE *BULLET* YOU BOUGHT *DIDN'T* KILL LAMONICA, MRS. HEWITT.

THE *SELLER* CLAIMED--

YEAH, HE *LIED.*

TELL YOU WHAT, WE'LL *TRADE* YOU FOR IT.

TRADE?

SURE. YOU WANTED A PIECE OF BLACK SPIDER MEMORABILIA, WELL, I'VE *GOT* ONE, AND IT'S *UNIQUE*...

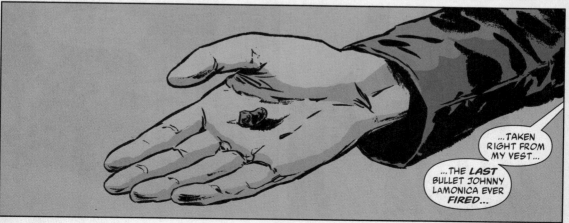

...TAKEN RIGHT FROM MY VEST...

...THE *LAST* BULLET JOHNNY LAMONICA EVER *FIRED*...

YOU'LL RUN THE *SLUG* DOWN TO THE *LAB* WHEN WE GET BACK.

YEAH, IF IT'S FROM ALLEN'S *GUN* LIKE WE FIGURE, THAT'LL BE THAT.

JUST KEEP IT AWAY FROM *CORRIGAN*, THAT'S ALL I *ASK*.

I SUSPECT CORRIGAN'S GONNA BE ON HIS *BEST* BEHAVIOR, EVEN *IF* THAT BOY'S ROTTEN TO THE *CORE*.

HE'S GONNA BE *UNTOUCHABLE*, NOW, YOU KNOW THAT.

ANYTHING YOU GET ON HIM, IT'S ALL FRUIT FROM THE *POISON* TREE.

I KNOW.

THEN *WHY'D* YOU TURN ME LOOSE ON HIM, INSPECTOR?

YOUR *PARTNER* WAS IN THE *JACKPOT*, MONTOYA. I COULDN'T LET THAT *SIT*.

SO YOU LET ME *KILL* YOUR *CASE* AGAINST CORRIGAN TO GET HIM OUT?

I DON'T *BELIEVE* YOU.

WHY'D YOU DO IT?

BECAUSE I *OWED* YOU ONE.

LET'S GIVE YOUR PARTNER THE *GOOD* NEWS.

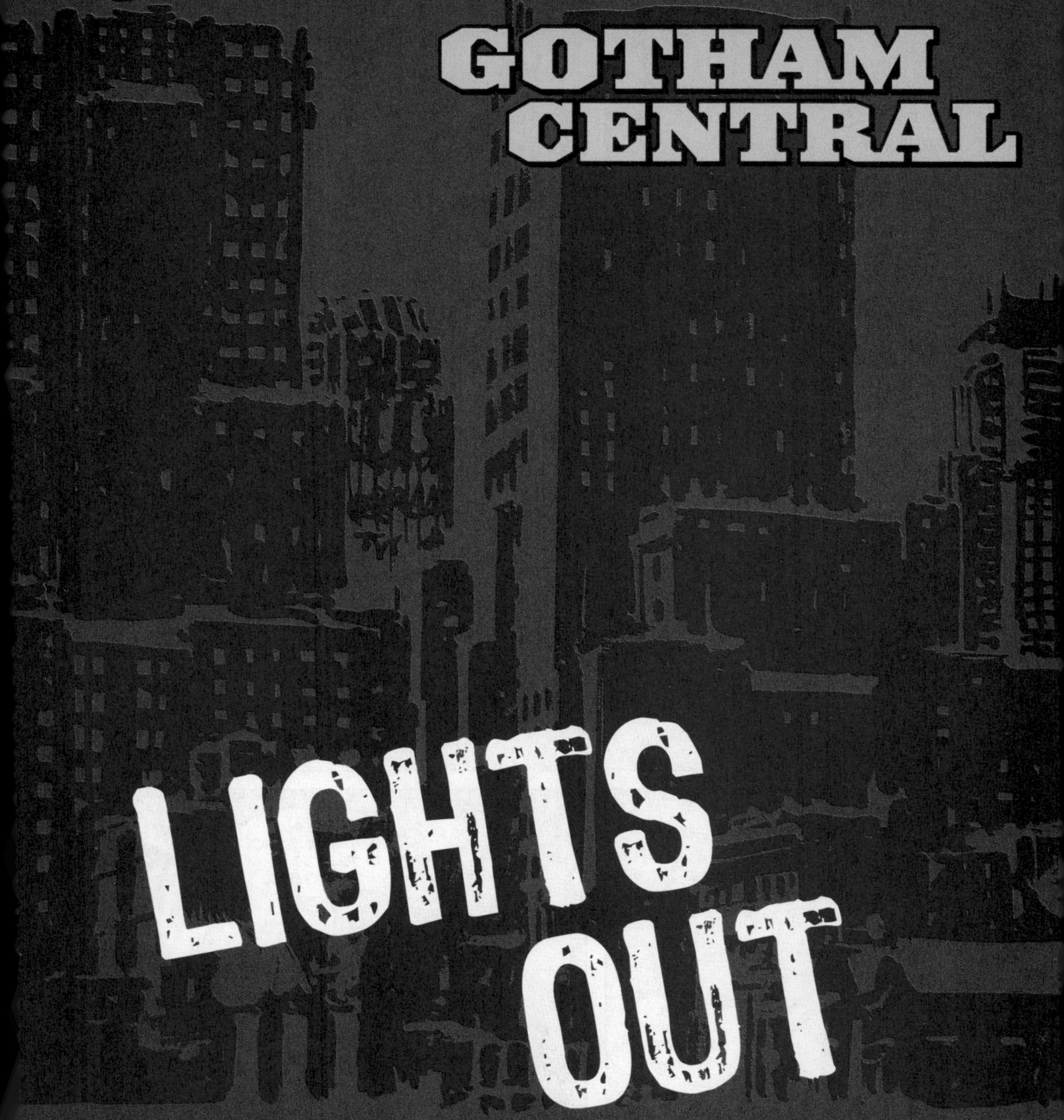

GOTHAM CENTRAL

LIGHTS OUT

GREG RUCKA
WRITER

MICHAEL LARK
PENCILLER

STEFANO GAUDIANO
INKER

JUST *THREE* OF YOU?

THE *WORK* ORDER SAID IT WAS *ROUTINE* MAINTENANCE, COMMISSIONER.

YOU *WANT*, I CAN GO BACK OVER TO CITY HALL AND MAKE A *REQUEST* FOR MORE.

AND HOW *LONG* WILL *THAT* TAKE?

WELL, YOU'D HAVE TO FILL OUT THE E-SEVENTY-TWO *AGAIN*, AND THEN A *SUPPLEMENTAL* FORM, Y'KNOW, *EXPLAINING* THE *CHANGE*...

FIGURE, MAYBE TWO, THREE WEEKS?

NO, I'M NOT *WAITING* ANY *LONGER*.

I WANT THIS *DONE* BY *TONIGHT*.

THEN ALL YOU GOT TO DO IS *TELL* US WHAT THE *JOB* IS.

THAT.

TAKE IT DOWN.

I WANT IT *GONE* BY NIGHTFALL.

HEY, WAIT A *SECOND!*

WHAT?

WHAT DO WE DO WITH IT WHEN WE'RE *DONE?*

I DON'T GIVE A DAMN.

I THINK *AKINS* IS OFF HIS *NUT*.

WELL, HE HASN'T *FIRED* YOU YET, SO THERE'S *EVIDENCE* TO *SUPPORT* THAT THEORY, TOMMY.

THANKS, DAG. THAT'S THE KIND OF *BACKUP* I WAS HOPING FOR FROM MY *PARTNER.*

SERIOUSLY, MAN, WHAT'S HE *THINKING,* TAKING THE *SIGNAL* DOWN AND ALL?

LIKE IT'S GONNA STOP THAT *LUNATIC* FROM *MESSING* IN OUR *BUSINESS* ANYWAY.

THE COMMISSIONER IS MAKING A *STATEMENT,* DETECTIVE BURKE...

...*ANNOUNCING* IN NO UNCERTAIN TERMS THAT THE G.C.P.D. AND THE BATMAN ARE NO LONGER ON SPEAKING TERMS.

MAYBE.

OR MAYBE HE'S JUST *ANNOUNCED* TO EVERY *INMATE* AT ARKHAM THAT GOTHAM IS NOW *EASY PICKINGS.*

WHICH CAME *FIRST?*

THE *BATMAN* OR THE *FREAKS?*

THE BATMAN IS ONE OF THE FREAKS.

SOMETHING THAT YOU NATIVE GOTHAMITES SEEM TO FORGET.

NO, HE'S NOT.

NO?

NO. HE SAVES LIVES. HE PROTECTS THE PEOPLE WE CAN'T.

YEAH, HE SAVED LOTS OF LIVES WHEN HE TOOK OVER THE POLICE BAND.

HE DID A BANG-UP JOB WHEN WE HAD BLACK MASK SURROUNDED.

HOW MANY COPS DIED IN THIS GANG WAR? TWENTY-SIX? TWENTY-SEVEN?

MORE THAN THAT.

OFFICER ACEDILLO DIED LAST NIGHT FROM THE INJURIES HE GOT IN ROBINSON PARK.

THAT SOUND LIKE A HERO TO YOU, RENEE?

BECAUSE I'M PRETTY SURE ROMY WOULD DISAGREE.

NICE SHOT, THERE, CRIS.

SHOVE IT, BURKE.

CAPTAIN SAWYER! MAGGIE! MAGS!

MAGS?

DIDN'T *LIKE* THAT ONE, HUH?

WHAT CAN *I* DO FOR YOU, SIMON?

YOU CAN *SLOW* DOWN FOR A START.

MAKE IT *FAST*, I'VE GOT SOME-WHERE TO BE.

EARLY *LUNCH*?

DOCTOR'S APPOINTMENT.

WHAT DO YOU *NEED*?

YOU GOT A *COMMENT* ABOUT WHAT'S GOING ON UP ON THE *ROOF*?

STACY **ALWAYS** HAS LUNCH UP THERE, SIMON. UNLESS THE **WEATHER'S** BAD.

SERIOUSLY.

THE **DEPARTMENT** HAS NO **OFFICIAL** COMMENT OR **POSITION** ON BATMAN, AND THAT **INCLUDES** THE **SIGNAL**, YOU KNOW THAT.

YEAH, I **KNOW** THE POLICY.

I'M ASKING FOR A **COMMENT** OFF THE **RECORD.**

IT'D HAVE TO BE **WAY** OFF THE RECORD.

HAVE I **EVER** TREATED YOU OR YOUR PEOPLE **WRONG,** CAPTAIN?

YOU **KNOW** I DON'T GIVE UP MY **SOURCES.**

YOU **KNOW** WHAT HAPPENED, SIMON.

HE **SCREWED** US.

WHAT **ELSE** IS AKINS SUPPOSED TO **DO?**

DUDE, CHECK *HER OUT...*

...WOULDN'T MIND GETTING SOME OF THAT.

HEY, SUGARLEGS!

HOPE YOU BROUGHT *ENOUGH* TO *SHARE*, SEXY!

C'MERE, I'LL *SHOW* YOU WHAT I *GOT* IN MY LUNCHBOX!

NAH, *DON'T GO!*

OW!

£#$%HOLE.

ROOF ACCESS AUTHORIZED PERSONNEL ONLY

...THEN JUST CUT OUT THE DAMN *MIDDLEMAN* AND START HANDING OUT *BADGES* TO THE GENERAL *POPULACE!*

WHAT YOU SEEM TO FORGET IS THAT THIS GUY IS A *VIGILANTE!*

AND THE DEPARTMENT'S *ENTIRE* RELATIONSHIP WITH THIS GUY WAS BUILT ON *ONE* SIMPLE *TRUST--*

AND HE *BROKE* IT!

YOU CAN'T *BLAME* HIM FOR *EVERY* LIFE THAT WAS *LOST,* CRIS!

I DON'T *HAVE* TO! ALL I HAVE TO DO IS BLAME HIM FOR *ONE!*

AND YOU'LL *FORGIVE* ME FOR SAYING THIS, *PARTNER,* BUT YOU'RE ABOUT AS OBJECTIVE ON THIS AS THE *POPE* IS ON THE SUBJECT OF *ABORTION.*

BITE ME, CRIS.

WHEN THE *POLICE* WORK WITH A *LAWBREAKER,* THE POLICE *LOSE* THE FAITH OF THE PUBLIC!

MAYBE YOU HAVEN'T NOTICED, BUT WE'VE NEVER *HAD* THE FAITH OF THE PUBLIC!

HE'S *NOT* A COP, HE'S *NEVER* BEEN A COP--

AND *THINKING* HE WAS ON OUR *SIDE* GOT PEOPLE *KILLED!*

59

JUST WHAT THE **HELL** ARE YOU **DOING?**

I BEG YOUR **PARDON,** MISTER MAYOR?

I ASKED WHAT THE **HELL** YOU'RE **DOING,** MIKE!

YOU DON'T MAKE A **DECISION** LIKE THIS WITHOUT **CONSULTING** WITH ME **FIRST!**

ASIDE FROM THE **FACT** THAT I LOOKED LIKE AN **ASS** AT THE **PRESS CONFERENCE** THIS MORNING, YOU DON'T HAVE THE **AUTHORITY** TO MAKE THIS KIND OF DECISION!

GCPD to Bat: Go to Hell!

Mayor Hull: "No Comment!"

YOU HAVE **ANY** IDEA HOW THIS MAKES ME **LOOK?**

NOT TO **MENTION** WHAT IT'S GOING TO DO TO THE **TOURISM** INDUSTRY IN THIS CITY?

I COULD CARE **LESS** ABOUT WHAT IT DOES TO **TOURISM.**

THIS IS ABOUT PROTECTING MY PEOPLE, AND BATMAN IS A **MENACE.**

YOU'RE THE COMMISSIONER OF POLICE, YOU HAD **DAMN** WELL BETTER CARE ABOUT **TOURISM!**

THE **HEALTH** AND **WELFARE** OF GOTHAM CITY IS YOUR **CONCERN,** COMMISSIONER.

PUT IT **BACK.**

NO.

YOU WANT ME TO *FIRE* YOU, MIKE? IS THAT WHAT YOU *WANT*?

BECAUSE I'LL BE *GLAD* TO DO IT.

I'VE GOT NO PROBLEM SENDING YOU *PACKING* AND FINDING ANOTHER *COP* WHO'LL ACTUALLY *LISTEN* TO ME.

THAT'S YOUR *CHOICE*.

BUT I'D THINK *TWICE* ABOUT MAKING A *MOVE* LIKE THAT, MISTER MAYOR...

...ESPECIALLY WHEN *MY* DEPARTMENT IS INVESTIGATING *YOUR* OFFICE FOR *CORRUPTION*.

WHAT? SINCE *WHEN*?

SINCE YOU TOOK THAT *LEXCORP-* SPONSORED *TRIP* TO THE *CAYMANS* AND LEFT *MRS. HULL* HERE AT *HOME*.

YOU WANT TO *CALL* MY *BLUFF*?

NO.

DIDN'T *THINK* SO.

NOW, YOU'LL *EXCUSE* ME...

...I'VE GOT AN *OFFICER'S* FUNERAL TO *ATTEND*.

...EASY...

...DAMMIT, I SAID EASY!

SORRY!

JUST WATCH THE SLACK, WILL YOU?

WE'RE GONNA SET IT OVER THERE, ALL RIGHT?

GOT IT.

JUST A LITTLE FURTHER...

AH, DAMMIT!

EVERY-
BODY ALL
RIGHT?

I'M FINE.

...YEAH,
THINK SO...

WHAT A
MESS.

WHAT A
MESS.

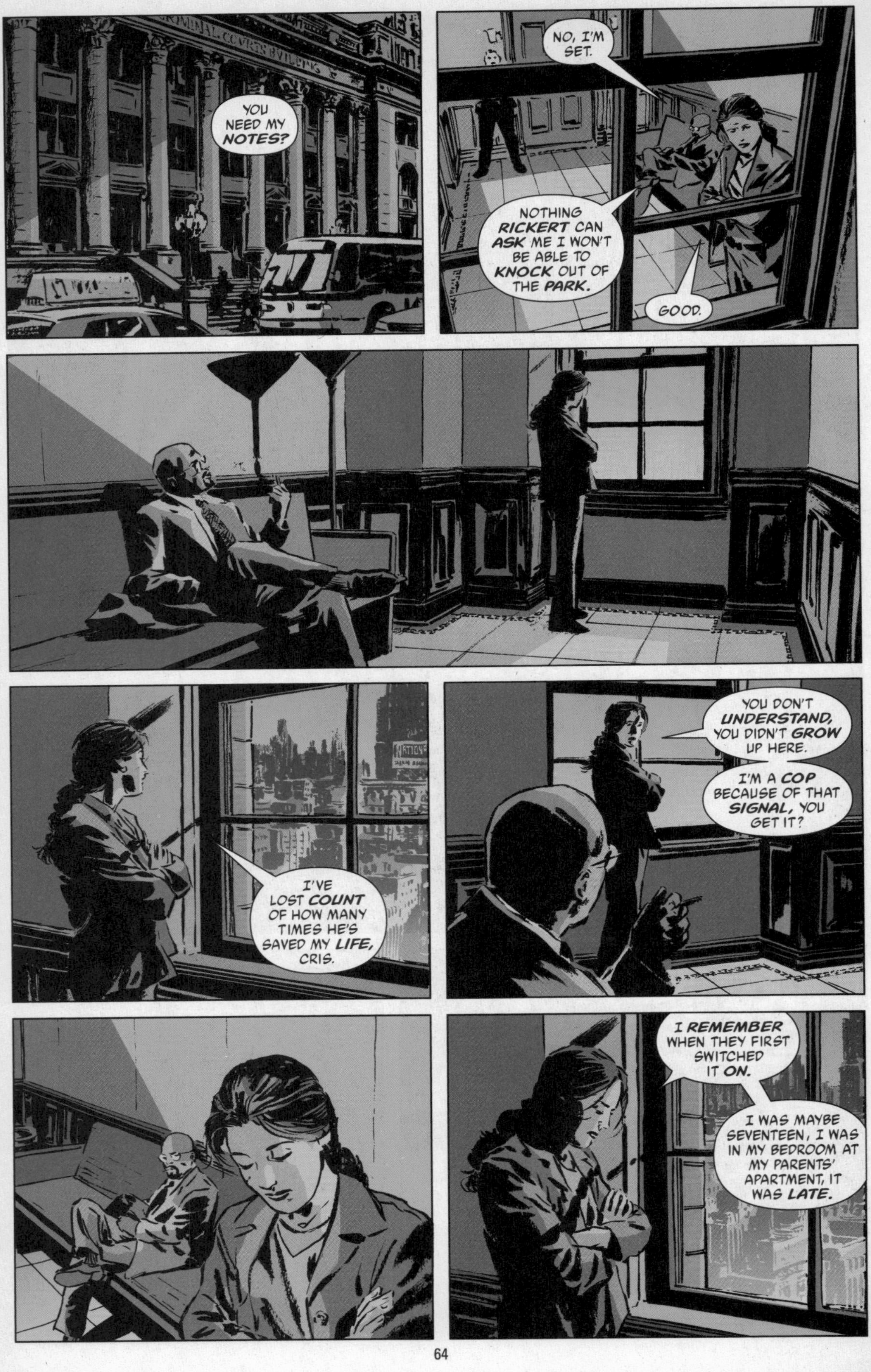
CRIMINAL COURTS BUILDING
YOU NEED MY NOTES?
NO, I'M SET.
NOTHING RICKERT CAN ASK ME I WON'T BE ABLE TO KNOCK OUT OF THE PARK.
GOOD.
I'VE LOST COUNT OF HOW MANY TIMES HE'S SAVED MY LIFE, CRIS.
YOU DON'T UNDERSTAND, YOU DIDN'T GROW UP HERE.
I'M A COP BECAUSE OF THAT SIGNAL, YOU GET IT?
I REMEMBER WHEN THEY FIRST SWITCHED IT ON.
I WAS MAYBE SEVENTEEN, I WAS IN MY BEDROOM AT MY PARENTS' APARTMENT, IT WAS LATE.

I WAS TRYING TO DO *HOMEWORK*, BUT I COULDN'T *CONCENTRATE*.

THERE'D BEEN THIS *STORY* IN THE *NEWS*, HOW THE *WATER SUPPLY* HAD BEEN *POISONED*.

EVERYONE IN THE *CITY* WAS *SCARED*.

I LOOKED OUT MY *WINDOW*.

DETECTIVE *ALLEN?*

YOUR *TURN* ON THE *STAND*.

RIGHT.

THANKS.

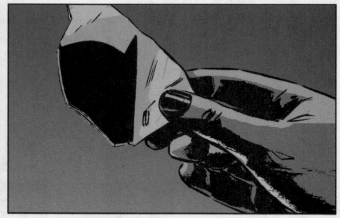

STACY?

CAPTAIN! I WASN'T--I MEAN, I DIDN'T...

IT'S ALL RIGHT.

BUT YOU CAN'T BE UP HERE.

NOT ANY-MORE.

I KNOW.

HE'S NOT A BAD GUY, CAPTAIN.

WE KNOW WHO THE BAD GUYS ARE, HE'S NOT ONE OF THEM.

I KNOW.

'NIGHT,
COMMISSIONER.

GOOD
NIGHT.

TURN
AROUND.

WONDERED
WHEN YOU'D
COME TO
BUST MY
CHOPS.

YOU'RE MAKING A *MISTAKE*.

FROM WHERE I'M *STANDING, I'M CORRECTING* ONE.

TAKING DOWN THE *SIGNAL* DOESN'T *CHANGE* ANYTHING.

I'LL *STILL* DO WHAT I NEED TO *DO*.

YOU MAY BE *RIGHT*.

BUT THIS WAY, AT LEAST, THERE WON'T BE ANY MORE CONFUSION.

THIS WAY, AT LEAST, MY PEOPLE WON'T MAKE THE MISTAKE OF THINKING THAT YOU'RE ON THEIR SIDE.

WE'RE ON THE SAME SIDE, COMMISSIONER.

NO, WE'RE NOT.

WE BOTH WANT TO PROTECT GOTHAM.

WE BOTH WANT TO KEEP ITS PEOPLE SAFE.

THAT'S WHAT I WANT.

BUT I DON'T THINK THAT'S WHAT YOU WANT.

WHAT ELSE COULD THERE BE?

I DON'T KNOW.

I DON'T KNOW WHY YOU DO WHAT YOU DO. IF IT'S ABOUT POWER OR EGO OR REVENGE...

...MAYBE JUST FOR KICKS...

FRANKLY, I DON'T CARE ANYMORE.

THE SIGNAL WAS THERE BECAUSE ONCE UPON A TIME THE G.C.P.D. TRUSTED YOU. WELL...

...THAT TIME HAS PASSED.

YOU **WON'T** STOP ME FROM **DOING** WHAT I NEED TO **DO.**

BATMAN, IF **WHAT** YOU NEED TO **DO** CONFLICTS WITH **MY** PEOPLE OR MY DEPARTMENT...

...IF IT **THREATENS** THEIR **LIVES** OR MY **AUTHORITY**...

...THEN **NOT** ONLY WILL I **STOP** YOU...

...I'LL **DESTROY** YOU.

YOU'LL **TRY.**

I'LL **SUCCEED.**

THEN LET'S **HOPE** THAT DAY **NEVER** COMES.

AMEN.

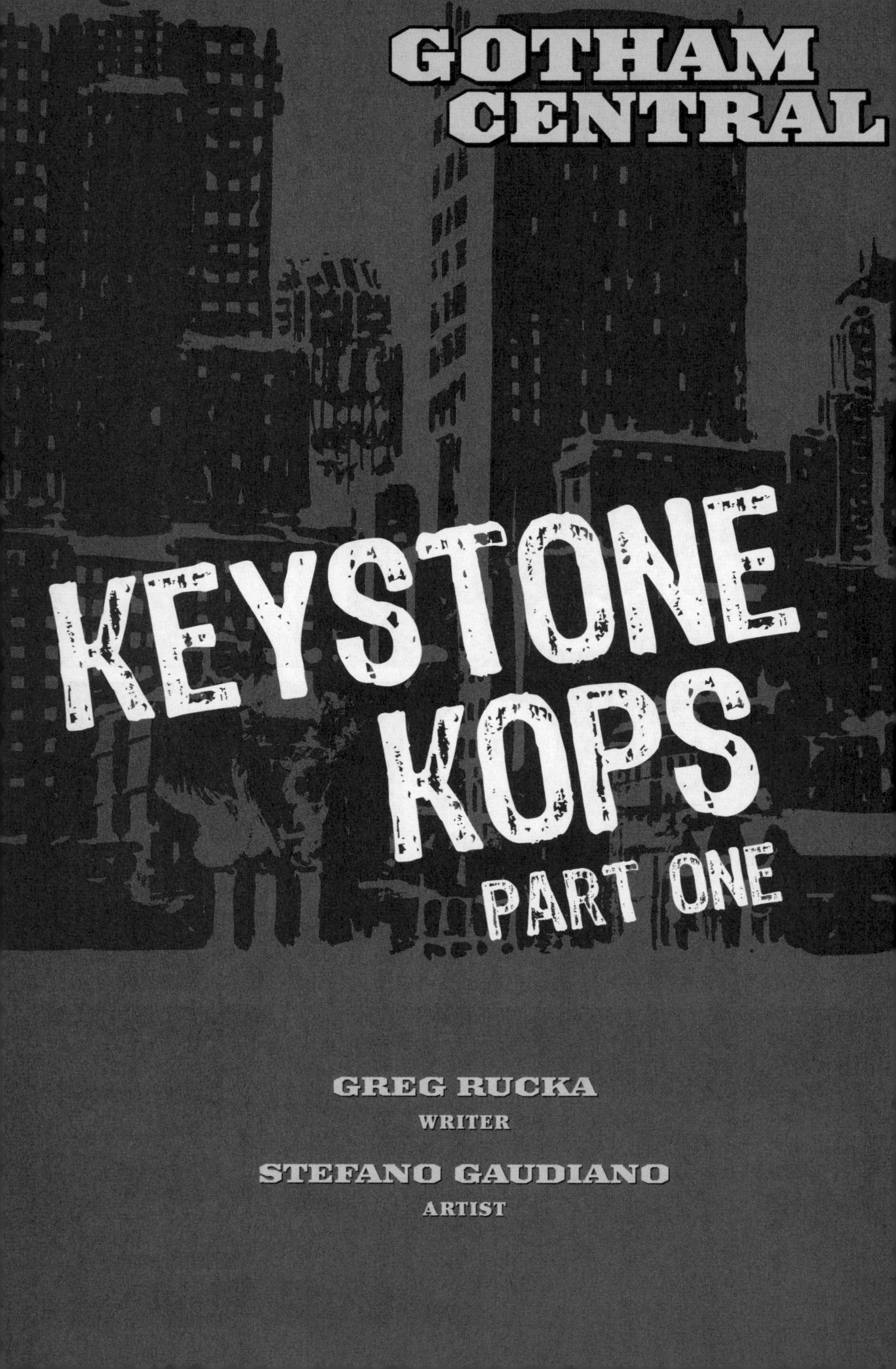

GOTHAM CENTRAL

KEYSTONE KOPS

PART ONE

GREG RUCKA
WRITER

STEFANO GAUDIANO
ARTIST

⟨...YOU'RE GONNA **HELP** ME WITH THE **HOMEWORK**, RIGHT?⟩

⟨...MY PARENTS WON'T EVEN LET ME **WATCH** IT, THEY SAY IT'S **TOO VIOLENT**--⟩

⟨--BUT I **DIDN'T,** HE SAID I **DID,** SO NOW I GOTTA WRITE THE **WHOLE** THING **AGAIN!**⟩

IT WAS **SICK** THE WAY YOU **FACED** JESUS, MAN! TOTALLY PUT HIM **DOWN!**

DON'T **SAY** THAT, MAN. I WASN'T LOOKING FOR ANY **TROUBLE.**

⟨MIGUEL! WAIT UP!⟩

⟨C'MON, ANNA, **HURRY,** WOULD YOU?⟩

I'LL CATCH YOU LATER, MIGUEL.

SEE YOU TOMORROW.

⟨MAMA SAYS YOU'RE SUPPOSED TO **WAIT** FOR ME, SHE SAYS YOU'RE SUPPOSED TO WALK **WITH** ME ALL THE WAY **HOME.**⟩

⟨I **AM** WALKING WITH YOU.⟩

⟨YOUR **LEGS** ARE **TOO** LONG! SLOW DOWN!⟩

⟨YOU GOTTA KEEP **UP!**⟩

⟨WE **HURRY,** WE CAN WATCH SOME CARTOONS BEFORE MAMA GETS HOME--⟩

⟨YOU BETTER HOPE YOUR MAMA'S *WAITING*, MIGUEL, 'CAUSE *YOU'RE* GONNA *NEED* HER.⟩

⟨JESUS... C'MON, MAN--⟩

⟨SHUT *UP!* YOU TALK LIKE *THAT*, LIKE WE'RE *FRIENDS*, YOU LITTLE *PUNK?*⟩

⟨WE'RE *NOT* FRIENDS, *FRIENDS* DON'T *RAT* YOU *OUT*, DON'T GET YOU *EXPELLED!*⟩

⟨IT'S NOT *MY FAULT* YOU HAD A *KNIFE* AT SCHOOL!⟩

⟨IT'S NOT *MY* FAULT YOU *PULLED* IT OR THAT THEY *TOOK* IT FROM YOU!⟩

⟨GOOD THING I GOT ME A *NEW* ONE, THEN, HUH?⟩

⟨WHICH EYE SHOULD I *TAKE*, YOU PIECE OF ¢*%$#?⟩

NGHH!

⟨ANNA! RUN TO *MONTOYA'S!* STAY THERE!⟩

RUN!

MIGUEL!

...TWENTY-THREE CENTS BACK.

THANKS, MISTER MONTOYA.

I DUNNO, ANDY, I THINK IT'S *ACID REFLUX* OR SOMETHING.

YOU SHOULD HAVE IT CHECKED *OUT*, DON. THAT'S A *SERIOUS* MEDICAL--

HELP! SOMEONE *PLEASE* HELP--

--IT'S JESUS, HE'S TRYING TO *KILL* MY *BROTHER*--

EASY, SWEET-HEART--

--HE'S TRYING TO KILL MIGUEL!

PLEASE, YOU'VE GOT TO *HELP* HIM!

WHICH WAY, HON?

IT WAS AROUND THE CORNER, THEY WENT AROUND THE CORNER--

STAY WITH MISTER MONTOYA.

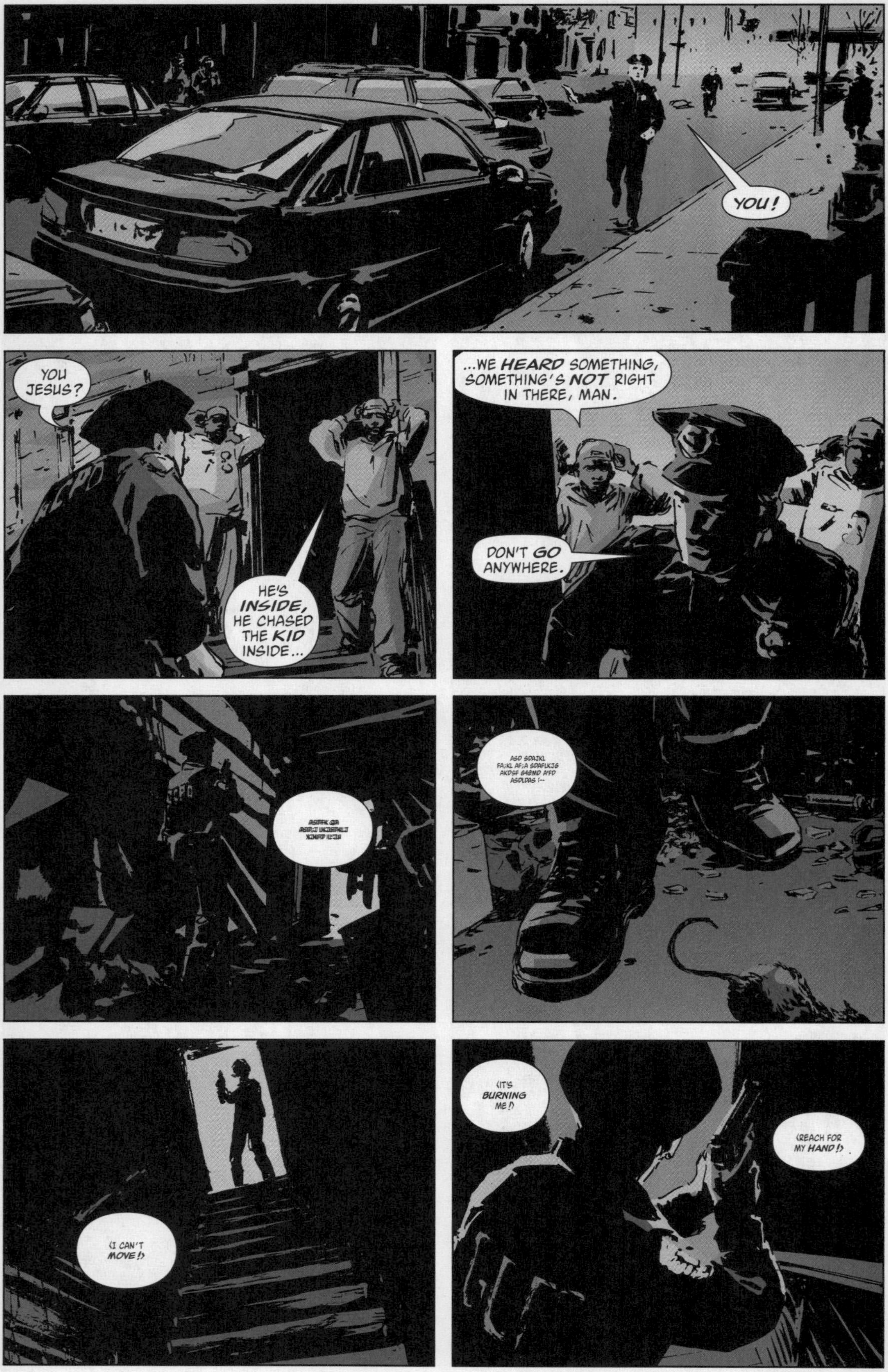
YOU!
YOU JESUS?
HE'S INSIDE, HE CHASED THE KID INSIDE...
...WE HEARD SOMETHING, SOMETHING'S NOT RIGHT IN THERE, MAN.
DON'T GO ANYWHERE.
‹I CAN'T MOVE!›
‹IT'S BURNING ME!›
‹REACH FOR MY HAND!›

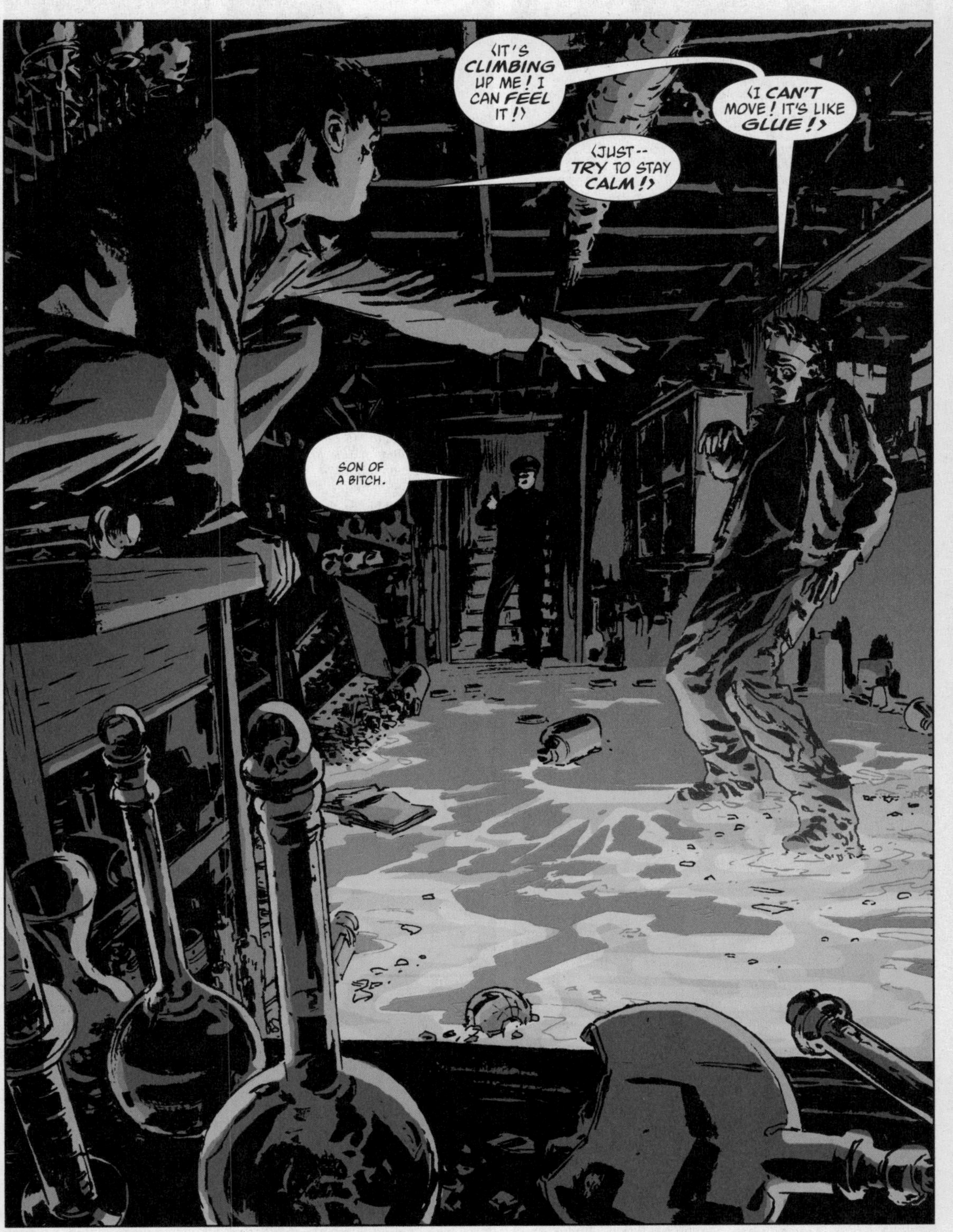
‹IT'S CLIMBING UP ME! I CAN FEEL IT!›
‹I CAN'T MOVE! IT'S LIKE GLUE!›
‹JUST-- TRY TO STAY CALM!›
SON OF A BITCH.

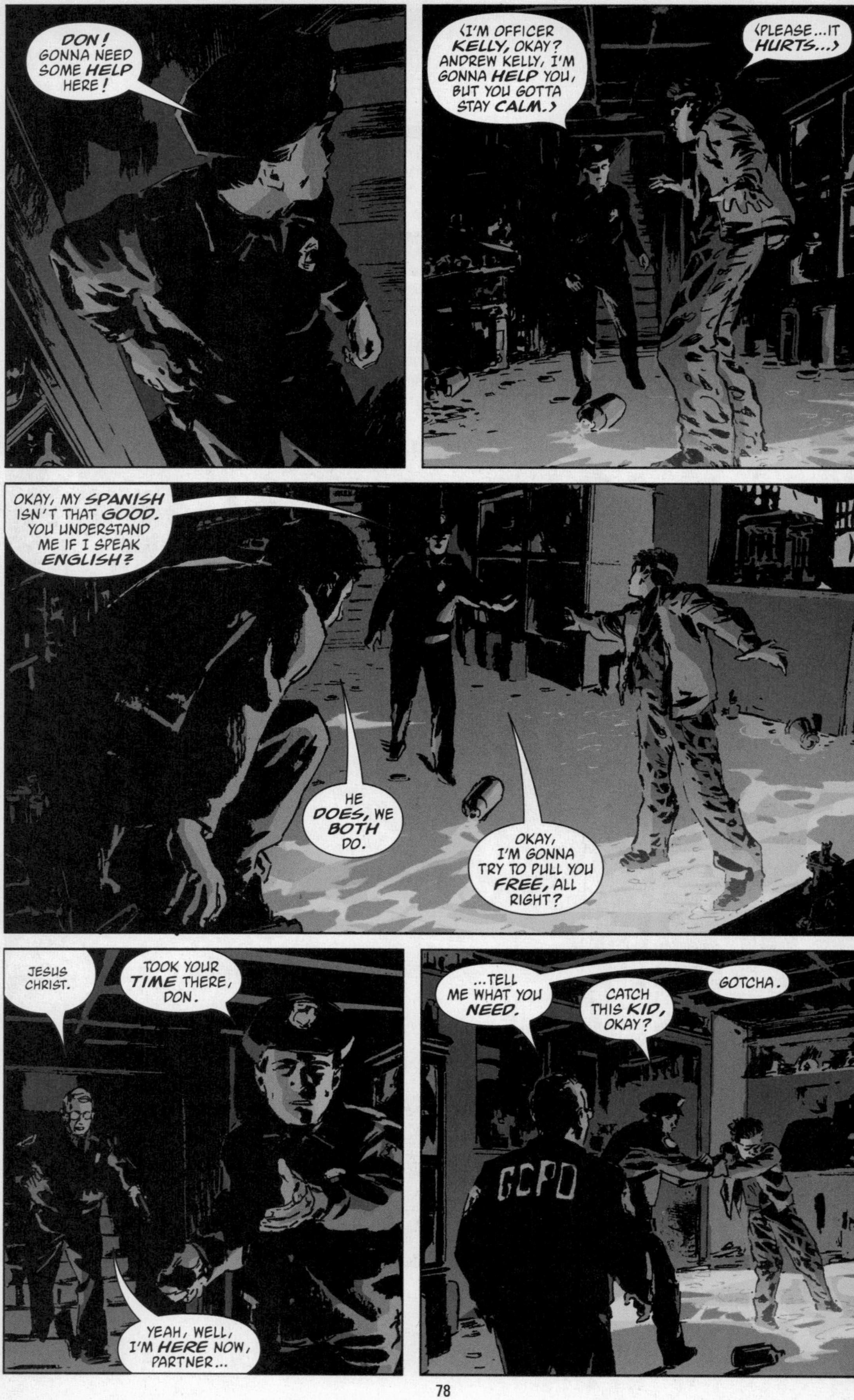
DON! GONNA NEED SOME HELP HERE!
‹I'M OFFICER KELLY, OKAY? ANDREW KELLY, I'M GONNA HELP YOU, BUT YOU GOTTA STAY CALM.›
‹PLEASE...IT HURTS...›
OKAY, MY SPANISH ISN'T THAT GOOD. YOU UNDERSTAND ME IF I SPEAK ENGLISH?
HE DOES, WE BOTH DO.
OKAY, I'M GONNA TRY TO PULL YOU FREE, ALL RIGHT?
JESUS CHRIST.
TOOK YOUR TIME THERE, DON.
YEAH, WELL, I'M HERE NOW, PARTNER...
...TELL ME WHAT YOU NEED.
GOTCHA.
CATCH THIS KID, OKAY?
GCPD

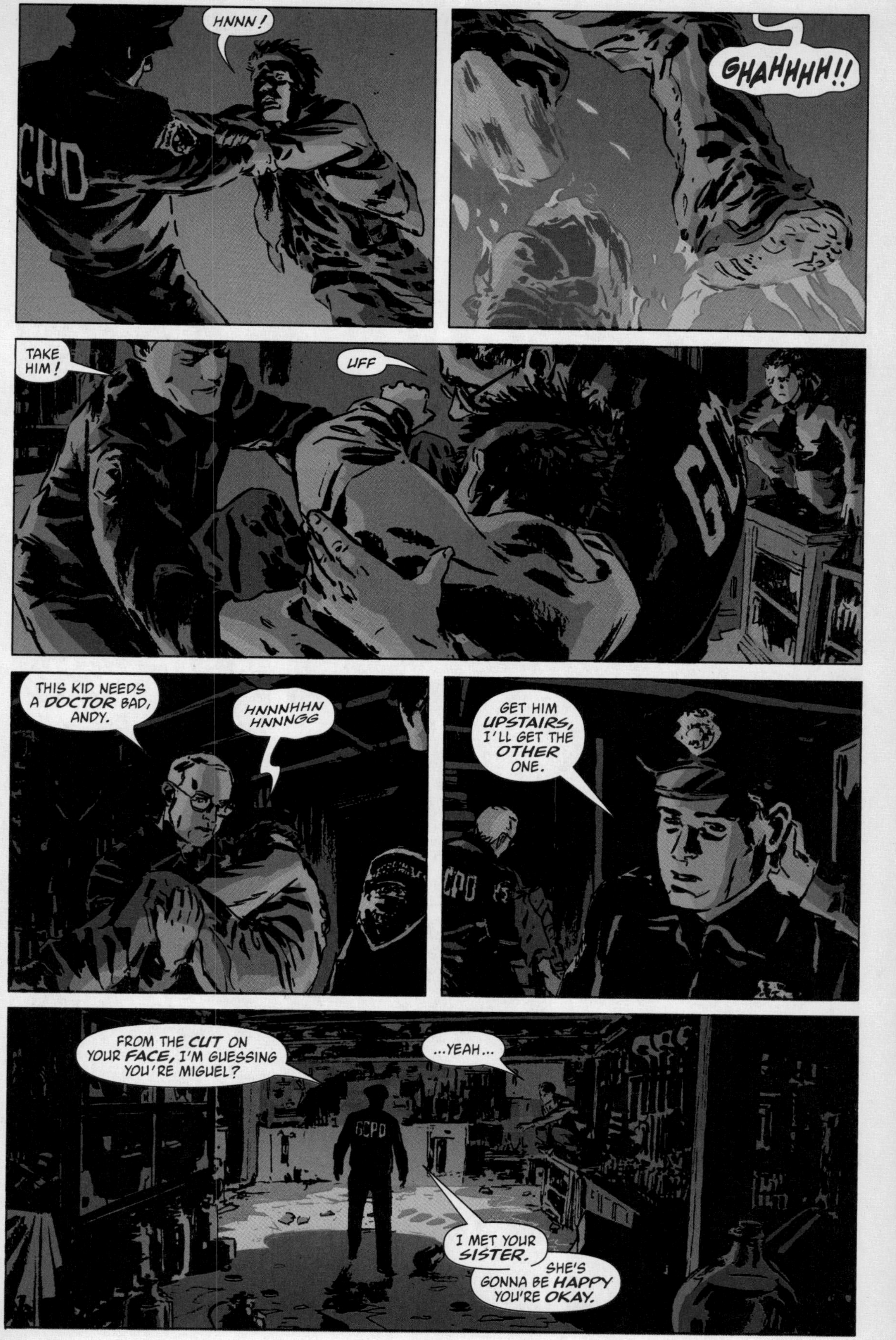
HNNN!
GHAHHHH!!
TAKE HIM!
UFF
THIS KID NEEDS A DOCTOR BAD, ANDY.
HNNNHHN HNNNGG
GET HIM UPSTAIRS, I'LL GET THE OTHER ONE.
FROM THE CUT ON YOUR FACE, I'M GUESSING YOU'RE MIGUEL?
...YEAH...
I MET YOUR SISTER.
SHE'S GONNA BE HAPPY YOU'RE OKAY.

YEAH. SHE'S KINDA A *PAIN*, THOUGH.

YEAH, I FEEL THE *SAME* WAY ABOUT *MY* KID SISTER.

OKAY, HERE'S WHAT WE'RE GONNA DO...

...YOU'RE GONNA *JUMP* TO ME, OKAY?

THAT WAY *NEITHER* OF US STEPS IN THIS *STUFF,* WHATEVER IT IS.

SAY *WHAT?*

YOU'RE GONNA *JUMP,* MIGUEL.

I'M GONNA *CATCH* YOU.

C'MON, *NEITHER* OF US WANTS TO *WALK* IN THIS STUFF, RIGHT?

I'LL KEEP YOU *SAFE.*

MY MAMA, SHE SAYS *COPS,* THEY JUST WANT *MONEY.*

YEAH. I'M *NOT* ONE OF *THOSE.*

YOU CAN *TRUST* ME. COME ON...

...YOU CAN *DO* IT...

KSSSH

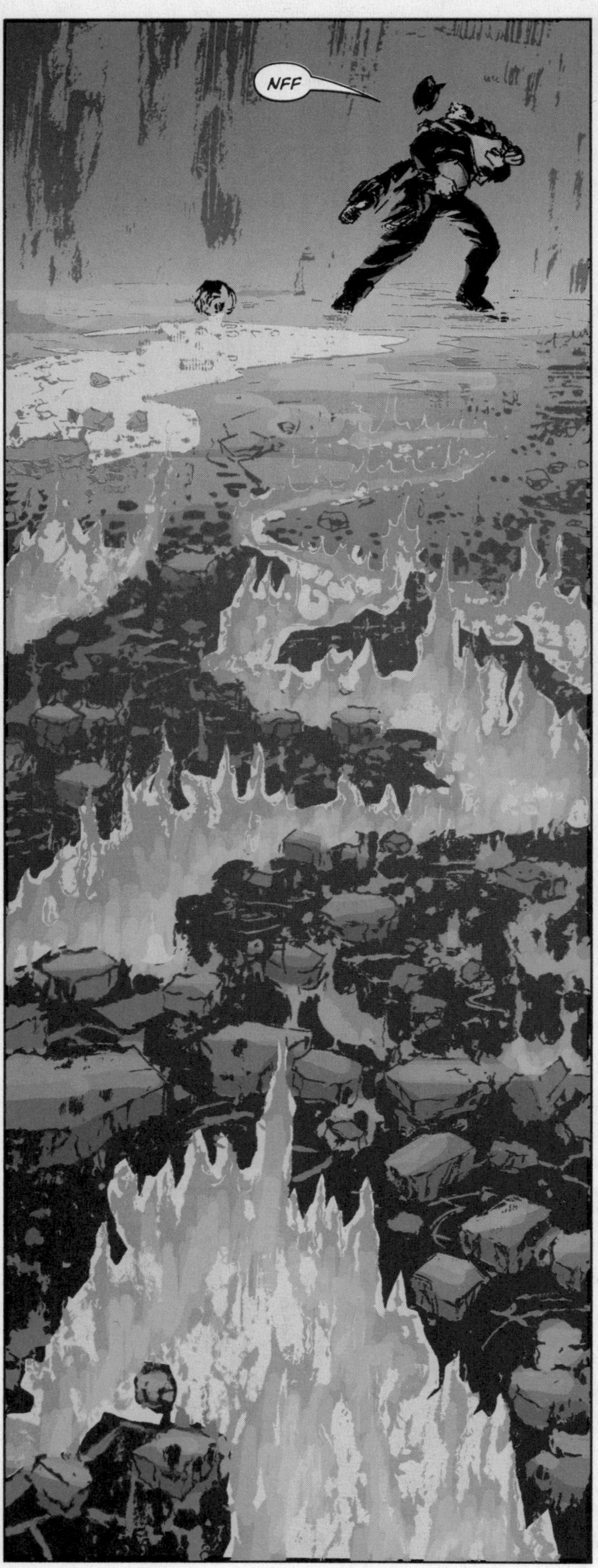
NFF

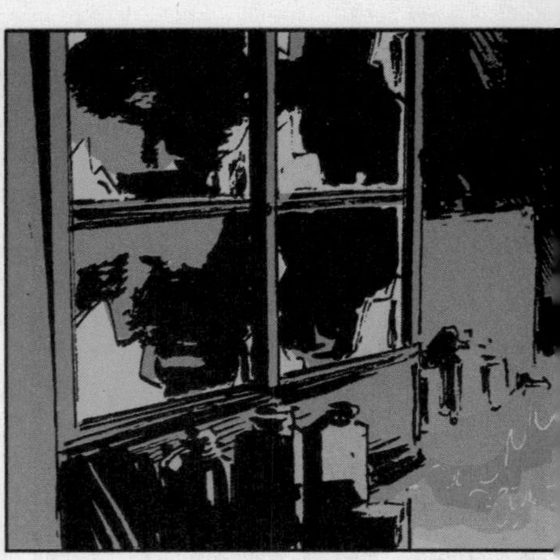

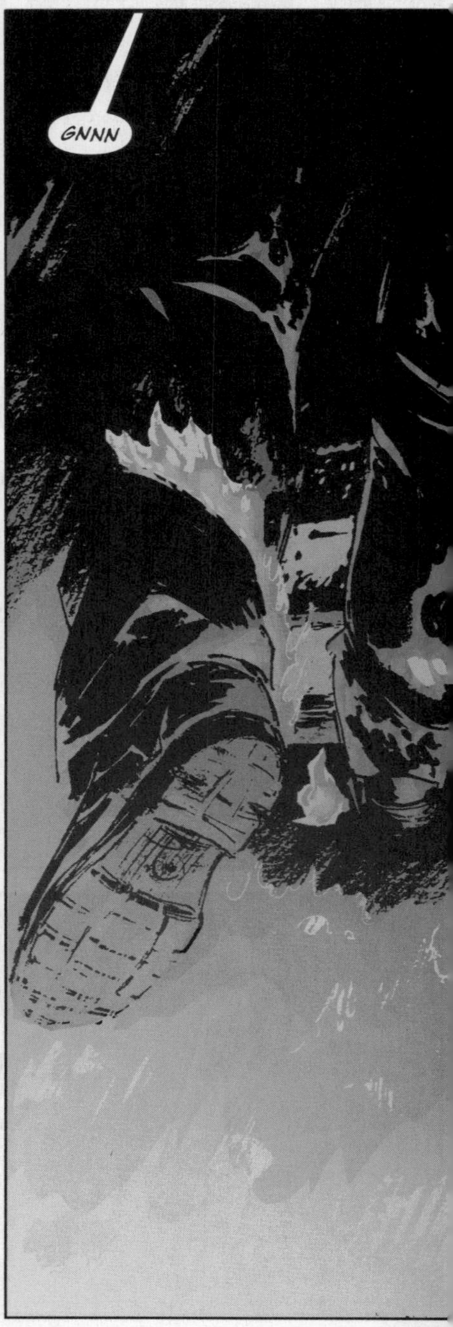
GNNN

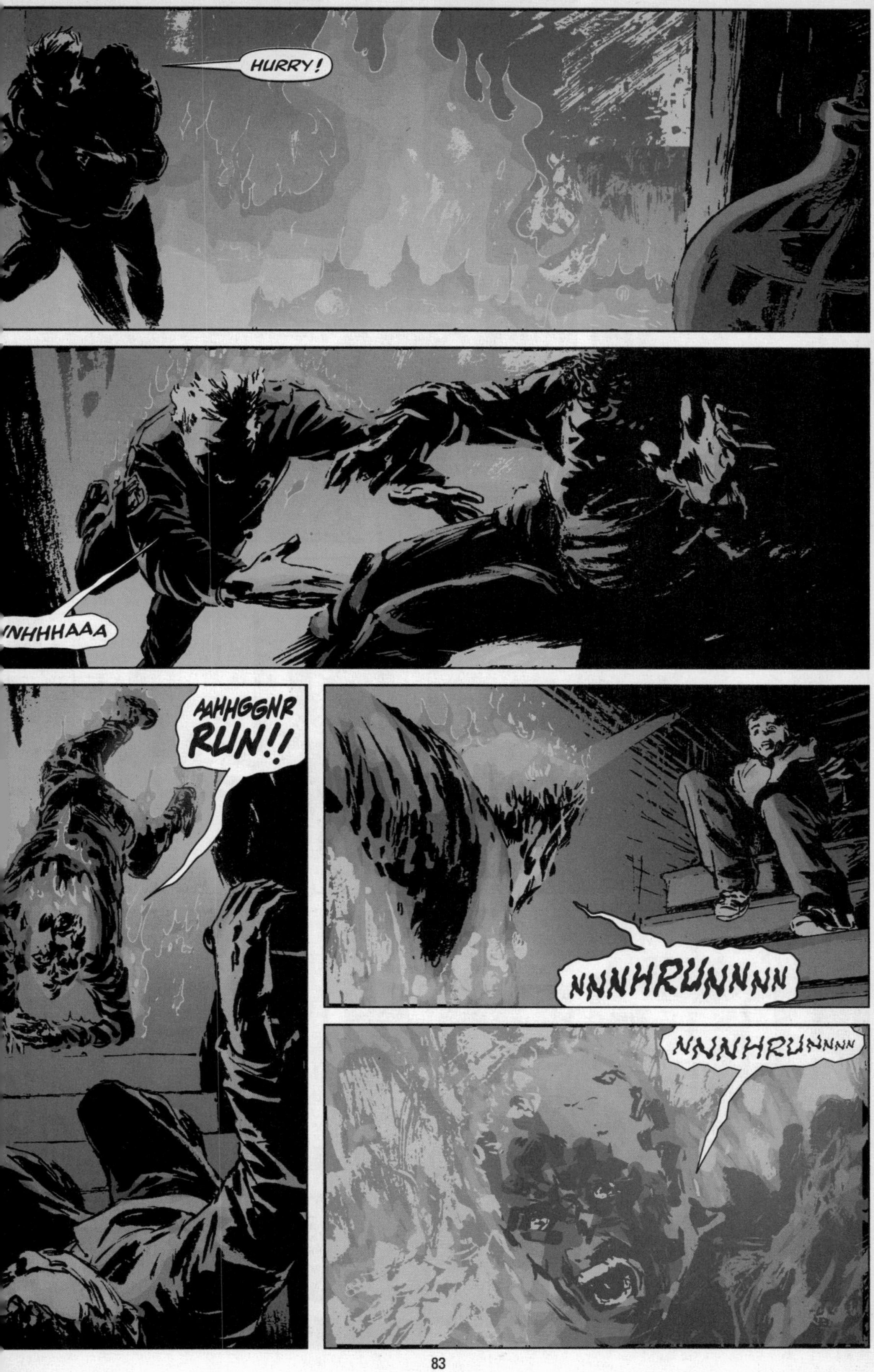
HURRY!
NHHHAAA
AAHHGGNR RUN!!
NNNHRUNNNN
NNNHRUNNNN

...BUT THE BEST THING ABOUT GETTING BACK ON DAYS...

...I GET TO SPEND TIME WITH MY KIDS AGAIN.

NOT TO MENTION DORE.

THAT, TOO.

WE'VE GOT TROUBLE...

...A UNIT WALKED INTO SOME FREAK'S HIDEOUT UP ON VAN BUREN AT A HUNDRED AND FIFTY-SIXTH.

ONE OF THE OFFICERS GOT FRIED, HE'S ON HIS WAY TO ST. LUKE'S.

DEL ARRAZIO, BARTLETT, IT'S YOURS.

WE GOT NAMES ON THE UNIT?

THEY'RE OUT OF THE NORTHERN, OFFICERS PEAK AND KELLY.

KELLY'S THE ONE GOT BURNED.

THEY DON'T THINK HE'S GONNA MAKE IT.

CAPTAIN, LET ME TAKE IT.

84

WHY SHOULD I DO THAT, RENEE?

I KNOW HIM.

WE CAME THROUGH NO MAN'S LAND TOGETHER.

NO. SERGEANT, GET UP THERE AND LET ME KNOW WHAT YOU FIND.

WILL DO, CAPTAIN.

LET ME **HAVE** IT.

YOU HAVE A **REASON** TO THINK SERGEANT DEL ARRAZIO CAN'T **HANDLE** IT, DETECTIVE, I'D BE **INTERESTED** IN HEARING IT.

HE **DOESN'T** KNOW HIM.

ASIDE FROM THE FACT THAT DEL ARRAZIO WAS **HERE** DURING N.M.L., IT WOULD SEEM TO ME **NOT** KNOWING OFFICER KELLY IS A **BONUS** IN THIS SITUATION.

THAT'S **NOT** THE THING, CAPTAIN.

IT'S...THAT'S **MY** OLD **NEIGHBORHOOD**. KELLY...

...I GOT HIM **STARTED** ON THE **JOB** AFTER N.M.L....

...I WAS HIS **RABBI**, Y'KNOW?

PLEASE, **MAGGIE**...

...I'VE NEVER ASKED YOU FOR **ANYTHING** BEFORE...

ALL RIGHT.

BUT **ALLEN** IS THE PRIMARY.

YOU **HEAR** ME? I SAID **ALLEN** IS THE PRIMARY!

I'LL KEEP YOU **POSTED**.

...THAT'S WHEN I GET DOWN TO THE *BASEMENT.* SWEAR TO *GOD,* IT'S LIKE SOMETHING OUT OF A *JOKER* PLOT, THERE'RE *TEST TUBES* AND ALL THAT #$¢*.

JOKER'S *STILL* IN ARKHAM.

I'M SAYING IT WAS *NUTS,* DETECTIVE, THAT'S *ALL* I'M SAYING.

THE *FIRST* KID, WE GET HIM *OUT*--HE'S THE ONE THAT HAD THE *KNIFE*--I BRING HIM UP, CALL FOR AN *AMBO.* START BACK *IN...*

...RUN INTO *THAT* ONE COMING UP THE STAIRS, SCREAMING ABOUT ANDY, HOW HE'S *BURNING* ALIVE.

THAT'S *IT.*

ANY WORD ON ANDY?

HE'S AT ST. LUKE'S, THAT'S ALL WE KNOW.

I'D LIKE TO HEAD OVER THERE.

YEAH, GO *AHEAD.*

OH, FOR %$¢*!S SAKE.

VINCENT!

87

YOU TALKED HER *INTO* IT?

SHE GAVE IT TO *ME*, YEAH.

MEANING SHE GAVE IT TO CRIS.

YOU'VE GOT *NO* DISTANCE ON THIS CASE, RENEE, YOU KNOW THAT.

LIKE *YOU* GOT *NO* DISTANCE WHEN YOU'RE WORKING ANYTHING WITH *INZERILLO* IN ITS *NAME*.

BUT I'VE *NEVER* DOUBTED YOU DID THE JOB *RIGHT* WHEN IT WAS ALL SAID AND *DONE*.

YOU WANT US TO INTERVIEW THE *WITNESSES* OR HEAD OVER TO THE *HOSPITAL*?

SEE WHAT YOU CAN GET FROM THE *WITNESSES*.

START WITH THE *GUY* WITH THE *MUSTACHE* AND THE *APRON*...

...HE KNOWS *EVERYBODY* IN THE *NEIGHBORHOOD*.

YEAH? HOW DO YOU KNOW *THAT*?

TRUST ME, I *KNOW*...

...HE'S MY *DAD*.

MAYBE YOU SHOULD TAKE THIS OPPORTUNITY TO *REBUILD* SOME *BRIDGES,* RENEE.

THEY DISOWNED *ME,* REMEMBER?

UNLESS IT'S TO *TELL* HIM I'M SUDDENLY *STRAIGHT...*

...THAT SON OF A BITCH DOESN'T WANT TO HEAR *ANYTHING* I HAVE TO SAY.

IT'S *MIGUEL*, RIGHT?

I DON'T KNOW IF YOU *REMEMBER* ME, I'M *RENEE*.

YOU'RE MISTER *MONTOYA'S* DAUGHTER. YOU'RE THE *COP*.

YEAH, I'M A *DETECTIVE*. THIS IS MY *PARTNER*, HIS NAME IS *CRIS*.

CAN YOU TELL ME WHAT *HAPPENED* IN THERE, MIGUEL?

JESUS...JESUS *CHASED* ME, HE HAD A *KNIFE*. I *RAN* INTO THE BUILDING, THEN *DOWN* THE *STAIRS*...

...THE *BASEMENT*, IT LOOKED LIKE THE *CHEMISTRY* LAB AT *SCHOOL*, THERE WERE ALL THESE *BEAKERS* AND *TEST TUBES*...

...I--I *KNOCKED* SOME *OVER* AND THEY *BROKE* AND IT *CAUGHT* JESUS, IT MADE HIM GET *STUCK*.

THE *COP* CAME, HE GOT US *OUT*...

〈...IT'S *MY FAULT!*〉

〈THE *COP* PICKED ME *UP*, BUT I KNOCKED THE *TUBE* OVER AND IT *BROKE* AND IT MADE THE *FIRE!*〉

〈TELL ME ABOUT THE *FIRE*, MIGUEL.〉

〈IT WAS...IT *WASN'T* LIKE *REAL* FIRE, RENEE! IT *BURNED*, BUT IT WASN'T *HOT*...〉

〈...IT'S *MY FAULT*...〉

〈...HE WAS TRYING TO *SAVE* ME...〉

NOT YOUR *AVERAGE* WEENIE ROAST.

TELL ME ABOUT IT.

INSPECTOR LANNING, G.C.F.D.

M.C.U. RENEE MONTOYA, THIS IS CRISPUS ALLEN.

WHAT CAN YOU *TELL* US?

JUST ABOUT *SQUAT*, HONESTLY. NEVER SEEN *ANYTHING* LIKE THIS.

LOOKS LIKE AN *AMMONIA* FIRE IN A LOT OF WAYS, BUT I'M NOT SEEING ANY OF THE *TRADITIONAL* HEAT SCARRING...

...*FIRE* CLIMBS, IT WANTS TO GO *UP*, YOU KNOW? BUT THESE *WALLS* ARE CLEAN, IT'S LIKE IT HUGGED THE *FLOOR* AND NEVER *ROSE*.

NOT EVEN *SMOKE* STAINS HERE.

MIGUEL-- THE KID OUTSIDE-- SAYS IT *BURNT* BUT THERE WAS NO *HEAT*.

KID'S A **MORON**, IT'S **NOT** POSSIBLE.

HE'S A **GOOD** KID, I KNOW HIS **MOTHER**.

YOU CAN SPEND CHRISTMAS WITH HIS FAMILY ALL I CARE, HE **STILL** DOESN'T KNOW WHAT HE'S **TALKING** ABOUT.

FIRE GENERATES **HEAT**, THAT'S THE WAY--

HEY...

COULD YOU MAYBE **SHINE** THAT **LIGHT** AT MY FEET INSTEAD OF AT MY **FACE**, LANNING?

YOU GOT SOME-THING?

YEAH, MAYBE...

...LOOKS LIKE THE **PERIODIC** TABLE...

THE **WHAT?**

THE **ELEMENTS**, YOU KNOW, IT WAS ON THE WALL OF YOUR CHEMISTRY CLASS IN HIGH SCHOOL?

I **CUT** CHEM.

...WHO THE *HELL* IS ALBERT DESMOND?

LET'S FIND *OUT.*

STACY? RENEE. BRING UP THE NVAC, RUN THE NAME *ALBERT DESMOND,* WOULD YOU?

THAT'S *WRONG,* THOSE ELEMENTS *DON'T* EXIST.

TECHNICALLY THEY *DO.* THEY JUST HAVEN'T BEEN *DISCOVERED* YET.

LOOKS LIKE *THIS* GUY THINKS HE'S A *GENIUS.*

HE *DOES.*

ALBERT DESMOND, A.K.A. *DOCTOR ALCHEMY.*

HE'S CURRENTLY A *GUEST* OF THE *STATE* AT IRON HEIGHTS, OUTSIDE OF KEYSTONE CITY...

...HE'S A MEMBER OF THE *ROGUES.*

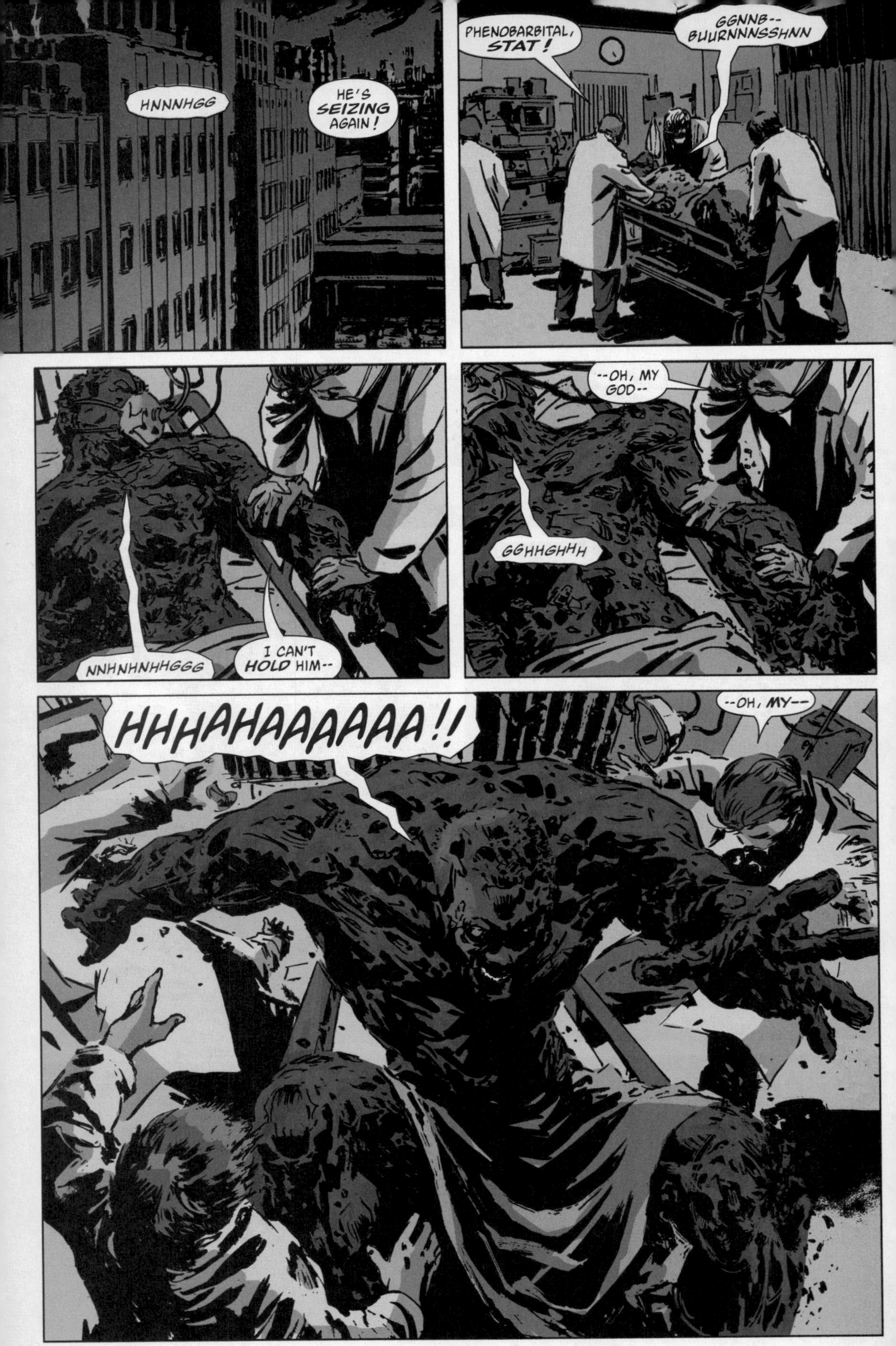
HNNNHGG
HE'S SEIZING AGAIN!
PHENOBARBITAL, STAT!
GGNNB-- BUURNNNSSHNN
NNHNHNHHGGG
I CAN'T HOLD HIM--
--OH, MY GOD--
GGHHGHHH
HHHAHAAAAAAA!!
--OH, MY--

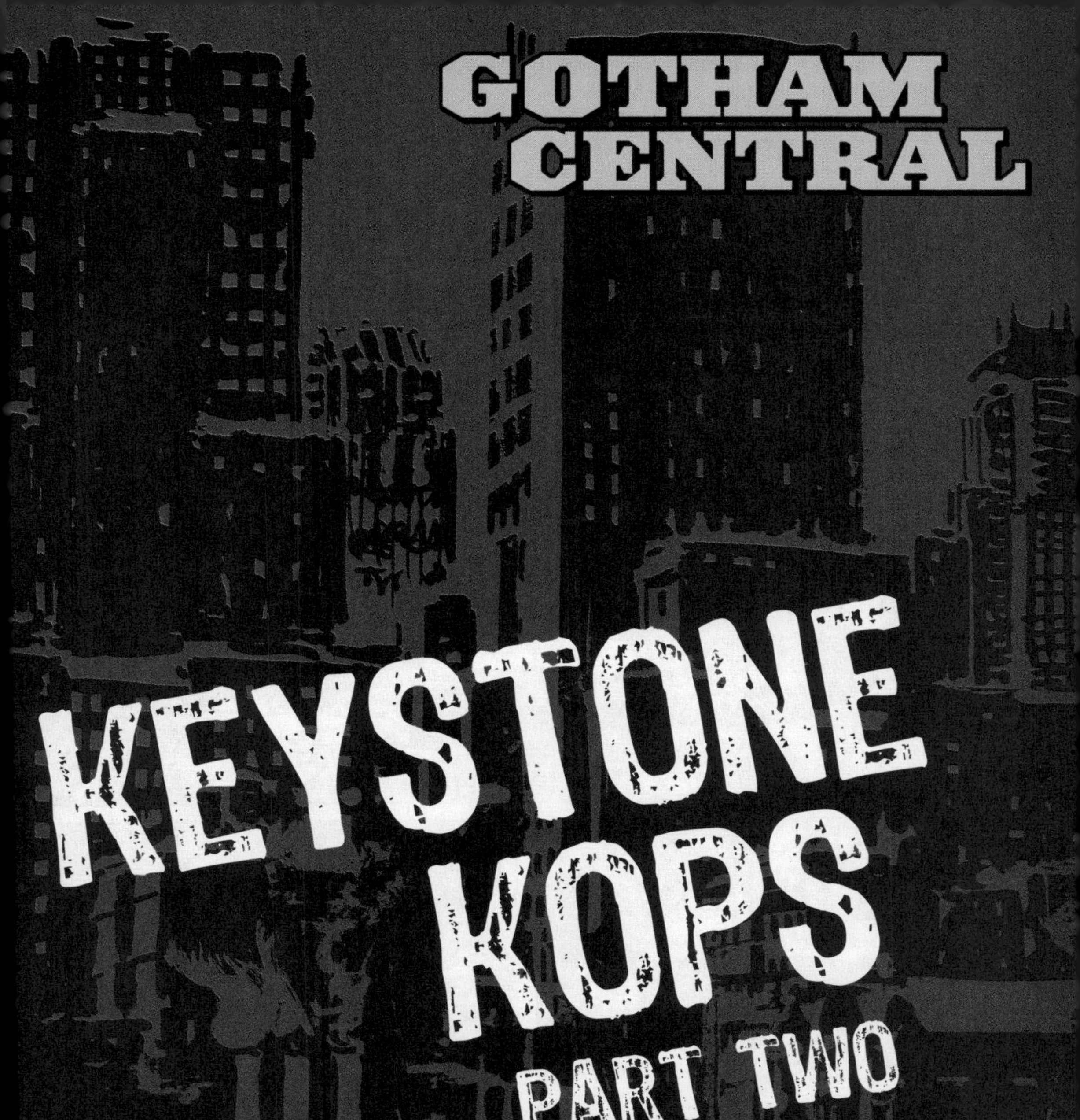

GOTHAM CENTRAL

KEYSTONE KOPS

PART TWO

GREG RUCKA
WRITER

STEFANO GAUDIANO
PENCILLER

KANO
INKER

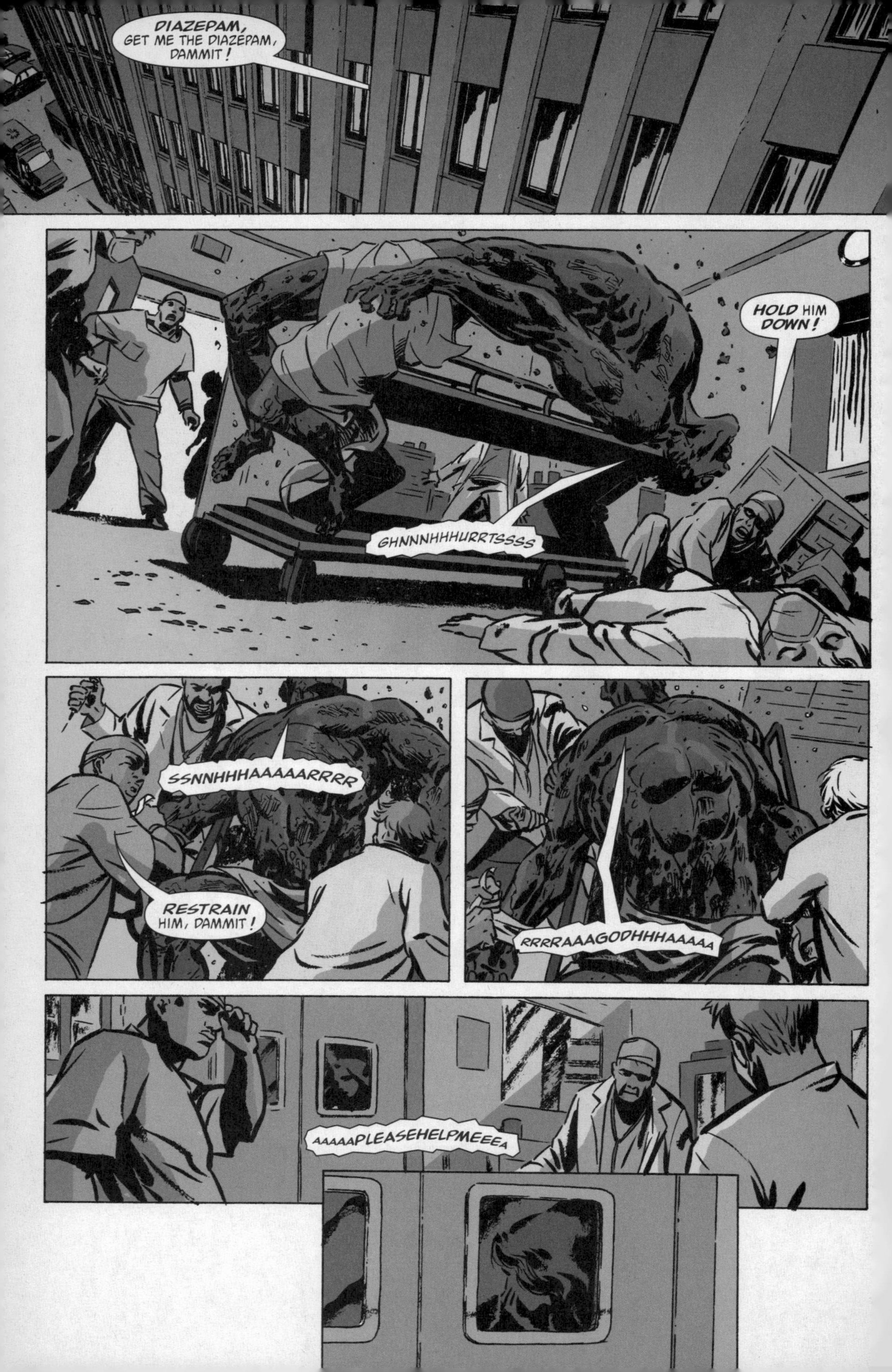
DIAZEPAM, GET ME THE DIAZEPAM, DAMMIT!
HOLD HIM DOWN!
GHNNNHHHURRTSSSS
SSNNHHHAAAAARRRR
RESTRAIN HIM, DAMMIT!
RRRRAAAGODHHHAAAAA
AAAAAPLEASEHELPMEEEA

HHNNHNNRAAA

SHARON?

SHARON!

OH, MY GOD, DON--

AAAARRHHGNNN

--SOMETHING'S *HAPPENING* TO HIM, SOMETHING'S HAPPENING TO ANDY!

GNNGHHNNN

HE KEEPS *SCREAMING*, DON.

HE *KEEPS* SCREAMING...

NNHHAAAHAAANN

HE DOESN'T *STOP*...

NNH HNNHN HNN

WE NEED TO **CHASE** THIS **DOCTOR ALCHEMY** THING DOWN.

LET'S HEAD **BACK**, THEN, DO IT FROM **CENTRAL**.

YEAH, THAT'S... ...DAMMIT...

CAN YOU GET A LIFT BACK WITH VIN AND JOE?

I NEED TO **DO** SOMETHING ELSE **FIRST.**

YOU **SURE** YOU WANT TO DO IT **ALONE?**

I THINK I'LL BE ALL RIGHT, THANKS.

YOU'RE A GOOD PARTNER, CRIS.

DING DING

WE'RE ABOUT TO *CLOSE*, SO PLEASE MAKE IT FAST.

HEY, PAPI.

‹I ALREADY SPOKE TO YOUR *FELLOW* DETECTIVES.›

‹I DON'T KNOW *WHAT* I CAN TELL *YOU* THAT I DIDN'T ALREADY TELL *THEM.*›

‹IF YOU'LL *EXCUSE* ME, I HAVE TO CLOSE UP NOW.›

‹I HAVE TO GET HOME FOR *DINNER.*›

‹SURE.›

〈SORRY TO HAVE **BOTHERED** YOU.〉

〈HEY.〉

〈ARE YOU...〉

〈...ARE YOU **STILL** SEEING THAT **GIRL**?〉

〈HER NAME'S **DARIA**.〉

〈WE'VE BEEN LIVING **TOGETHER** FOR ALMOST A **YEAR** NOW.〉

〈OH.〉

DING DING

101

--NO, MAN, IT'S **CHANGING** HIM **SOMEHOW,** SOME **MAD SCIENTIST** $#%€.

WHATEVER KELLY WALKED **INTO,** DEFINITELY A **FREAK** THING.

MAYBE WE CAN START **TAKING** THOSE PEST BASTARDS **DOWN** PERMANENT-LIKE NOW THAT WE GOT THE **BAT** OUT OF OUR--

HEY, **MONTOYA** !

DETECTIVE, HOLD UP A SEC !

MAKE IT FAST, **DOGNAVICH.**

YOU'RE WORKING THE VAN BUREN **CALL?** THE ONE THAT **BURNED** KELLY?

I AM.

YOU **FIND** THE **FREAK** WHO DID IT, YOU LET US **KNOW,** DETECTIVE, OKAY?

I MEAN...MAYBE WE **PATROL** SLOBS DON'T HAVE A LOT OF **LOVE** FOR YOU **THINKERS** IN THE M.C.U., BUT KELLY'S A **GOOD** POLICE...

...YOU GOT **HALF** THE COPS IN THE WESTERN **BREAKING** HEADS TONIGHT, TRYING TO FIND THE S.O.B. WHO HURT OUR **BOY.**

TRYING TO **FIND** THE MOTHER*€%#* BEFORE **YOU** GUYS DO.

YOU **UNDER-STAND** WHAT I'M SAYING?

I **UNDER-STAND**.

WE'RE ON THE **SAME** PAGE HERE, RIGHT?

WE'RE IN THE **SAME** SENTENCE, DOG.

YOU **FIND** THE PERP...

...I'LL **HELP** YOU HOLD THE SON OF A BITCH **DOWN**.

--YOU HAVE *ONE* OF THEM CALL ME, THEY GET THE MESSAGE, OKAY?

YEAH, DETECTIVE CRISPUS ALLEN, G.C.P.D., MAJOR CRIMES UNIT...

TAKE A *LOOK.*

WHAT IS IT?

MY MAN MARCUS HERE PUT TOGETHER A LITTLE *DOSSIER* ON DOCTOR ALCHEMY...

...SEEMS OFFICER ANDREW KELLY HAS A *LOT* OF *FRIENDS.*

HE DOES.

CRIS? YOU GOT ANY-THING?

KEYSTONE P.D. IS CHECKING THAT ALBERT DESMOND IS *STILL* INCARCERATED AT IRON HEIGHTS.

GOT A LINE ON A DETECTIVE OUT THERE, NAME OF CHYRE, WAITING FOR A CALL *BACK.*

THERE *ANY* PHYSICAL EVIDENCE THAT *TIES* THIS WHACKO TO THE SCENE?

OTHER THAN THAT *PERIODIC TABLE?* NOTHING YET.

WAY THE *LAB* WORKS, IT'LL BE ANOTHER FEW *DAYS,* AND THAT'S IF WE'RE *REALLY* LUCKY, PARTNER.

NOT LIKELY.

JOELY, YOU HEAR FROM THE **HOSPITAL?**

YEAH. *NOT* GOOD, RENEE.

HE'S IN A *LOT* OF *PAIN.* SOMETHING'S *HAPPENING* TO HIS *BODY.*

THERE'S SOME *SPECIALIST* FROM S.T.A.R. GOTHAM TAKING A LOOK AT HIM NOW.

LIKE *THAT'LL* HELP.

BRRRT,T
BRRRT,T

M.C.U., ALLEN.

...YEAH, THAT'S RIGHT, THAT WAS ME...

...NO, IT'S *OFFICER-INVOLVED*...YES, EXACTLY...

...ALL RIGHT, THANK YOU, DETECTIVE.

KEYSTONE?

YEAH. DESMOND'S *STILL* LOCKED UP.

BEFORE HIS *LAST* GO-ROUND WITH THE *FLASH,* THOUGH, HE DISAPPEARED FOR A WHILE. MIGHT'VE BEEN WHEN HE CAME TO GOTHAM.

I THINK HE'S *OUR* GUY, RENEE.

NO QUESTION, I THINK HE'S OUR GUY.

...GO ON...

...IS THERE *ANY* WAY TO *REVERSE* IT?

...I SEE...

...YES, THANK YOU. KEEP ME INFORMED.

THAT ABOUT KELLY?

YEAH, WHATEVER IT IS, IT'S GETTING *WORSE*.

WHAT'S THIS?

THAT IS DOCTOR ALBERT DESMOND, CAP. *Ph.D.*s IN CHEMISTRY, BIOCHEMISTRY, MOLECULAR BIOLOGY--

--AND THE BAND PLAYS *ON*--

--CURRENTLY BEHIND *LOCK* AND *KEY* AT IRON HEIGHTS CORRECTIONAL, KEYSTONE.

HE FITS?

LIKE A *GLOVE*, CAPTAIN.

WE'RE THINKING WE NEED TO *TALK* TO HIM, AND *SOON*.

SOONER THAN YOU *THINK*.

I JUST GOT OFF WITH THE *ATTENDING* AT ST. LUKE'S.

KELLY IS **MUTATING**.

MUTATING HOW?

I LOOK LIKE THE **SPECIALIST** FROM S.T.A.R. LABS TO YOU, DETECTIVE ALLEN?

NO, MA'AM.

NOBODY **KNOWS**.

AND **NOBODY** KNOWS HOW TO **STOP** IT.

DESMOND DOES.

IT WAS HIS BOOBY TRAP. IF **ANYONE** CAN REVERSE IT, IT'LL BE DESMOND.

THAT ASSUMES HE'D **WANT** TO HELP US.

YOU THINK WE CAN **DEAL** WITH HIM?

DOUBT IT. DOUBT THERE'S **ANYTHING** WE CAN EVEN **OFFER** HIM.

WELL, YOU'RE GOING TO FIND **OUT**.

STACY!

CAPTAIN?

FIND OUT WHEN THE **FIRST** FLIGHT TO **KEYSTONE** IS IN THE MORNING...

...WE'RE GONNA NEED **TICKETS** FOR CRIS AND RENEE.

DEE, YOU HOME?

I'VE GOT TO GO TO KEYSTONE TOMORROW...

DEE?

KLK

KLK-KLK

DAMMIT.

KLK-KLK-KLK

HOLD IT--

--NHH!

DETECTIVE.

JESUS!

CAN'T YOU JUST SAY HELLO LIKE NORMAL PEOPLE?

DESMOND.

DON'T DEAL.

I WON'T ASK HOW YOU KNOW.

IF DESMOND CAN SAVE OFFICER KELLY--

HE CAN'T.

NO DEALS.

YOU DIDN'T USED TO BE SO COLD.

YOU WOULD KNOW.

KLK

THIS IS NEW. BEEN STANDING IN THE **DARK** FOR LONG?

NOT **TOO** LONG.

I **THINK** I'M **RELIEVED.**

SO JASON ORDERED TOO MUCH **SALMON** FOR THE **SPECIAL,** SO I THOUGHT I'D--

--WHOA, COWGIRL!

YOU'LL BE *BACK* TOMORROW NIGHT?

SHOULD BE.

BRING ME A *SOUVENIR,* ONE OF THOSE *FLASH* SHIRTS, SOMETHING LIKE THAT.

I'LL *TRY.*

WHAT IS IT?

I SAW MY FATHER. I WENT BY THE BODEGA, TRIED TO SAY HELLO.

HOW'D IT GO?

NOTHING'S *CHANGED.*

RENEE, DON'T DO THIS TO YOURSELF.

A YEAR AND A *HALF* AND *NOTHING'S* CHANGED, DEE. *NOTHING'S* CHANGED.

EXCEPT ME.

DADDY!!! --YOU, LOOK AT YOU! CAN' BELIEVE--

...DELA DIDN'T I'D MAKE THE CONNECTION...

SOMEONE'S MEETING US?

--THEN MY BELT, THEN MY SHOES, FOR GOD'S SAKE!

--NO IDEA HOW MUCH I MISSED YOU--

EXCUSE ME. I SAID, EXCUSE ME--

THAT'S WHAT STACY SAID.

THOSE TWO.

YEAH.

DETECTIVE CHYRE?

THAT'D BE ME. YOU'RE ALLEN?

CRISPUS ALLEN, YEAH...

...THIS IS MY PARTNER, RENEE MONTOYA.

JARED MORILLO.

NICE TO MEET YOU.

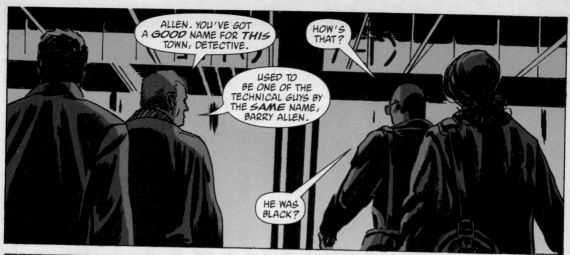

ALLEN. YOU'VE GOT A *GOOD* NAME FOR *THIS* TOWN, DETECTIVE.

HOW'S THAT?

USED TO BE ONE OF THE TECHNICAL GUYS BY THE *SAME* NAME, BARRY ALLEN.

HE WAS *BLACK?*

WHITE AS MICHAEL BOLTON.

HOPE YOU BOTH ARE WEARING YOUR *LONG JOHNS.* NO TELLING *WHEN* THIS STORM'S GOING TO END.

FORECAST THIS MORNING WAS FOR *CLEAR* AND COLD.

YEAH, THAT'S WHAT *WE'D* HEARD, TOO.

HOP IN, WE'LL HEAD STRAIGHT OUT TO *IRON HEIGHTS.*

WEATHER WIZARD'S *LOOSE,* COULD BE *HIM.*

CHYRE, TURN ON THE *HEATER.*

IT'S STILL *BUSTED.*

WEST SAID HE'D *FIX* IT.

GUESS HE DIDN'T HAVE THE *TIME.*

NO PARKIN JR STONE

YOU HEARD FROM OUR **CAPTAIN**?

THE **D.A.**s ARE **TALKING**. I THINK IT'S A **BAD** IDEA, THOUGH, CUTTING A **DEAL** WITH HIM.

DESMOND'S ONE OF THE **SMARTEST** OF THE **ROGUES**. NUTS, BUT **BRILLIANT**.

"ROGUES"?

YEAH, THEY'RE A GROUP OF **METAS**, WORK TOGETHER TO MAKE **OUR** LIVES **MISERABLE**.

CHRIST, THEY'VE **UNIONIZED**?

YOUR GUYS DON'T DO THAT?

GUNS AND **SHIELDS**, KIDS.

OUR GUYS **RARELY** COOPERATE.

I WENT OVER SOME CASE **FILES**. **DESMOND** COULD'VE RUN TO **GOTHAM** ABOUT EIGHTEEN MONTHS BACK.

PROBABLY WHEN HE SET THAT LITTLE **BOOBY TRAP** YOUR OFFICER FOUND.

DOCTOR ZOLOMON IS WAITING FOR YOU INSIDE.

THANKS, GEOFF.

ALL RIGHT, WE'RE GOOD. IT'S **THIS** WAY--

GIMME A SECOND.

DOCTOR ZOLOMON.

HMM?

THESE ARE THE DETECTIVES FROM GOTHAM.

RIGHT. ASHLEY ZOLOMON, I'M THE ROGUE PROFILER FOR THE KEYSTONE P.D.

YOU HAVE YOUR *OWN* STAFF PROFILER?

WE SHOULD GET ONE OF THOSE.

DOCTOR DESMOND HAS BEEN MOVED INTO SECURE *HOLDING* SO YOU CAN SPEAK WITH HIM.

I'LL REMAIN OUT HERE WITH DETECTIVES MORILLO AND CHYRE.

ALPHA HOLDING

IN ADDITION TO THE *OBVIOUS* SAFETY PROTOCOLS, YOU SHOULD KNOW THE *FOLLOWING* THINGS BEFORE YOU SPEAK TO HIM.

HE'S *BRILLIANT* AND *MANIPULATIVE.* HE WILL TRY TO MANIPULATE *YOU.*

THE THING HE *CARES* FOR *MOST* IS HIS *WORK.* HE DOES *NOT* CONSIDER HIMSELF A *CRIMINAL,* BUT RATHER A *SCIENTIST.*

APPEAL TO HIM AS A *MAN OF SCIENCE,* DETECTIVES...

ALPHA HOLDIN

...BUT BE *CAREFUL* THAT *YOU'RE* THE ONES MANIPULATING *HIM...*

NEW *FACES.*

THIS *IS* EXCITING.

" ...AND *NOT* THE OTHER WAY *AROUND.* "

AND FROM *FAR* AWAY.

GOTHAM CITY.

SOMEONE FOUND THE *EXPERIMENT,* THAT'S *IT,* ISN'T IT? EMBRACED MY *FIRES* OF *CREATION* AND THUS ARE THEY *CHANGED.*

AND HERE YOU STAND, SEEKING MY *WISDOM,* HOPING TO *COMPREHEND* THAT WHICH IS *BEYOND* YOUR KEN.

YOU *CAN'T.* DON'T EVEN *TRY.*

BUT ASK *NICELY,* AND PERHAPS I'LL *HELP* YOU ALL THE SAME.

GOTHAM CENTRAL

KEYSTONE KOPS

PART THREE

GREG RUCKA
WRITER

STEFANO GAUDIANO
PENCILLER

KANO
INKER

DOCTOR DESMOND, MY NAME'S DETECTIVE ALLEN. THIS IS MY *PARTNER* DETECTIVE MONTOYA.

THINK YOU CAN *ANSWER* A FEW *QUESTIONS* FOR US?

QUID PRO *QUO*, DETECTIVE ALLEN...

...OR FOR THOSE OF YOU *WEAK* WITH THE *LATIN*, "SOMETHING FOR SOMETHING."

TWO DETECTIVES COME ALL THE WAY FROM *GOTHAM* TO MINE MY *GRAY MATTER*, WHAT DO I GET IN *RETURN*?

DEPENDING ON YOUR *LEVEL OF COOPERATION,* THE WARDEN IS WILLING TO *OFFER* YOU CERTAIN *CONCESSIONS.*

ACCESS TO YOUR *RESEARCH,* FOR INSTANCE.

VERY GOOD, DETECTIVE ALLEN. NO *HINT* OF *HESITATION.*

BUT WE *BOTH* KNOW THAT YOU'RE LYING TO ME. WARDEN WOLFE WOULD NEVER ALLOW FOR SUCH AN *ARRANGEMENT.*

TRY *AGAIN.*

LET'S *HEAR* WHAT YOU'VE GOT.

THEN WE'LL DECIDE WHAT IT'S *WORTH* TO US.

TSK TSK TSK

DETECTIVE MONTOYA, *REALLY.* YOU KNOW HOW TO PLAY *BAD COP* BETTER THAN *THAT.*

IF YOU'RE **NOT** GOING TO BRING YOUR **BEST** GAME, I SEE NO **REASON** TO **PLAY** AT ALL.

SIT BACK DOWN.

OR WHAT? YOU'LL COME IN **HERE** AND **BEAT** ON ME? I **DOUBT** THAT.

I THINK I'LL ASK THE **SCREW** TO **RETURN** ME TO MY **CELL**.

DO THAT AND YOU **LOSE** YOUR CHANCE TO **PROVE** HOW MUCH **SMARTER** THAN US YOU **ARE**.

OH, **VERY** GOOD.

YOU'VE **KEPT** ME IN THE **ROOM**, WELL DONE. QUID PRO QUO, SOMETHING FOR SOMETHING.

BUT THAT **DOESN'T** BUY YOU **ANSWERS**.

THEN WHAT **DOES**?

YOU ASK **YOUR** QUESTIONS. THEN **I'LL** ASK **MINE**.

HONESTY **BREEDS** TRUST, DETECTIVES. BUT YOU LIE TO **ME**, AND I'LL **LIE** TO YOU.

AND I **WILL** KNOW IF YOU ARE **LYING**, BELIEVE ME.

YOU GO **FIRST**.

...AS OF SIX HOURS AGO, THE *MUTATION* SEEMS TO HAVE *STABILIZED.*

GOTHAM CITY, ST. LUKE'S HOSPITAL.

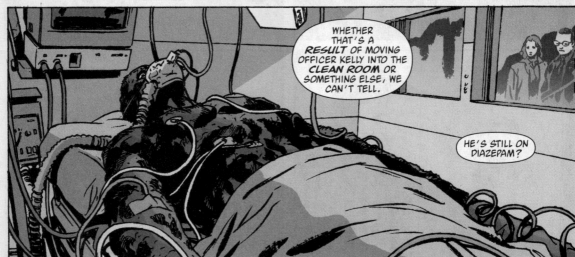

WHETHER THAT'S A *RESULT* OF MOVING OFFICER KELLY INTO THE *CLEAN ROOM* OR SOMETHING ELSE, WE CAN'T TELL.

HE'S STILL ON DIAZEPAM?

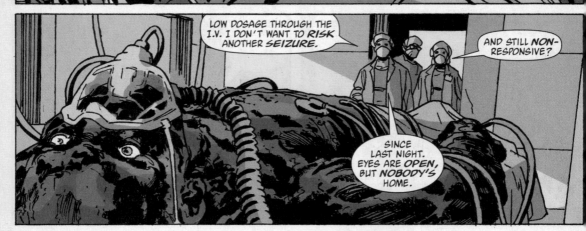

LOW DOSAGE THROUGH THE I.V. I DON'T WANT TO *RISK* ANOTHER *SEIZURE.*

AND STILL *NON-*RESPONSIVE?

SINCE LAST NIGHT. EYES ARE *OPEN,* BUT *NOBODY'S* HOME.

WHO'RE *THEY?* FAMILY?

SHE'S KELLY'S *GIRLFRIEND.* THE OTHER ONE IS HIS *PARTNER.*

THEY'RE *NOT* GOING TO WANT TO *WATCH* THIS.

CLOSE THE *BLINDS,* PLEASE.

YES, DOCTOR.

HEY...SHARON, NO, IT'LL BE ALL RIGHT.

ANDY'S TOUGH, HE'LL PULL THROUGH.

I DON'T...

...I DON'T UNDERSTAND!

WHAT'S HAPPENING TO HIM?

WHY WOULD SOMEONE DO THIS?

WHY?

I DON'T KNOW, HONEY.

I DON'T KNOW.

KNOWLEDGE, OF COURSE.

WHAT IS THE PURPOSE OF *ANY* EXPERIMENT, AFTER ALL?

MY TURN, NOW.

IS OFFICER--KELLY, IS IT?--IS OFFICER KELLY *STILL* UNDERGOING THE *TRANSFORMATION*, OR HAS THE *PROCESS* ARRESTED ITSELF?

LAST WE *HEARD* FROM THE HOSPITAL, HE'D *STABILIZED*.

OUR TURN.

THIS *EXPERIMENT* OR *TRANSFORMATION* OR *WHATEVER* YOU WANT TO CALL IT...

CAN IT BE *UNDONE*? CAN *YOU* UNDO IT?

THAT'S *TWO* QUESTIONS, DETECTIVE. THE ANSWER TO *BOTH* IS YES.

HMM... LOOK AT *YOU*... FRESH *SCAR* TISSUE ON YOUR *KNUCKLES* AND AROUND YOUR *EYE*...

...YOU SEEM TO HAVE DEVELOPED A *TASTE*--IF NOT A *DELIGHT*--FOR *VIOLENCE* RECENTLY, DETECTIVE.

I ALSO NOTE THE *DOUBLE VENUS* PENDANT YOU'RE WEARING AT YOUR *THROAT*...

...*GAY PRIDE* IS SUCH A *WONDERFUL* THING...

JUST ASK YOUR *DAMN* QUESTION.

IT'S A *KNOWN* FACT THAT INCIDENCES OF *DOMESTIC VIOLENCE* IN SAME-SEX RELATIONSHIPS IS QUITE *HIGH*. IT'S *ALSO* QUITE HIGH AMONGST *POLICE OFFICERS*.

SO MY *QUESTION* IS THIS:

DO YOU *BEAT* HER, DETECTIVE *DYKE*?

YOU SON OF A BITCH.

IS THAT A **YES**?

QUID PRO QUO, REMEMBER. TELL THE **TRUTH**.

RENEE--

HE EXPECTS ME TO **DIGNIFY** THAT, TO ACTUALLY **RESPOND** TO **THAT**?

WE NEED HIS **HELP**.

STATISTICALLY, INCIDENCES OF **DOMESTIC VIOLENCE** ARE **IDENTICAL** FOR STRAIGHTS AND GAYS, DOCTOR DESMOND--

YOU'RE **AVOIDING** MY QUESTION.

DO YOU **BEAT** HER, DETECTIVE?

NEVER IN MY **LIFE**.

HOW DO WE **CURE** KELLY?

YOU **DON'T**.

I **DO**.

AND THE **PENNY** DROPS.

HOW?

THAT I **CAN'T** ANSWER, I'M AFRAID, NOT UNTIL I **SEE** THE **EXPERIMENT**.

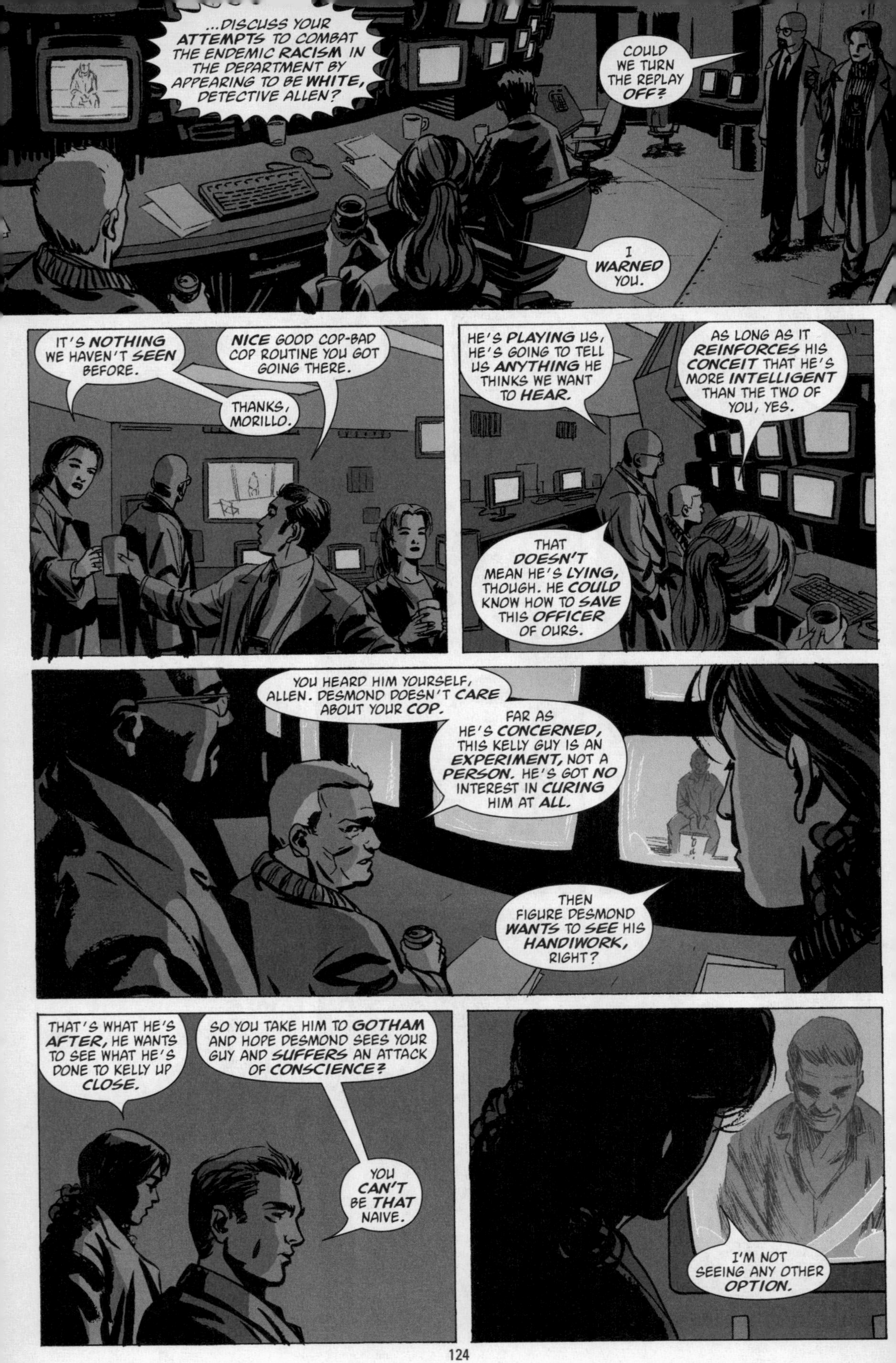
...DISCUSS YOUR ATTEMPTS TO COMBAT THE ENDEMIC RACISM IN THE DEPARTMENT BY APPEARING TO BE WHITE, DETECTIVE ALLEN?
COULD WE TURN THE REPLAY OFF?
I WARNED YOU.
IT'S NOTHING WE HAVEN'T SEEN BEFORE.
NICE GOOD COP-BAD COP ROUTINE YOU GOT GOING THERE.
THANKS, MORILLO.
HE'S PLAYING US, HE'S GOING TO TELL US ANYTHING HE THINKS WE WANT TO HEAR.
AS LONG AS IT REINFORCES HIS CONCEIT THAT HE'S MORE INTELLIGENT THAN THE TWO OF YOU, YES.
THAT DOESN'T MEAN HE'S LYING, THOUGH. HE COULD KNOW HOW TO SAVE THIS OFFICER OF OURS.
YOU HEARD HIM YOURSELF, ALLEN. DESMOND DOESN'T CARE ABOUT YOUR COP.
FAR AS HE'S CONCERNED, THIS KELLY GUY IS AN EXPERIMENT, NOT A PERSON. HE'S GOT NO INTEREST IN CURING HIM AT ALL.
THEN FIGURE DESMOND WANTS TO SEE HIS HANDIWORK, RIGHT?
THAT'S WHAT HE'S AFTER, HE WANTS TO SEE WHAT HE'S DONE TO KELLY UP CLOSE.
SO YOU TAKE HIM TO GOTHAM AND HOPE DESMOND SEES YOUR GUY AND SUFFERS AN ATTACK OF CONSCIENCE?
YOU CAN'T BE THAT NAIVE.
I'M NOT SEEING ANY OTHER OPTION.

I DON'T KNOW, MAYBE DESMOND *SEES* KELLY, SOMETHING SHAKES *LOOSE*.

SOME- THING WE CAN *USE*.

IF WISHES WERE *HORSES*.

PROBABLY WHY THERE AREN'T ANY HORSES IN GOTHAM.

YOU'LL *EXCUSE* US, WE NEED TO MAKE A COUPLE OF *CALLS*.

THINK WE CAN GET THE *DEPARTMENT* TO SPRING FOR *TWO* TICKETS TO *GOTHAM*?

YOU WANT TO *BABYSIT* THIS *DISASTER-IN-THE- MAKING*?

THEY'RE GONNA GIVE THAT *LUNATIC* JUST WHAT HE *WANTS*.

THAT *DOESN'T* MEAN *THEY* WON'T GET WHAT *THEY* WANT IN *TURN*, DETECTIVE CHYRE.

ALBERT DESMOND IS--TO PUT IT *BLUNTLY*--AN *ARROGANT BASTARD*.

HE *LIKES* TO *GLOAT*, AND IF THEY GIVE HIM *ENOUGH* ROPE, THERE'S A CHANCE DOCTOR ALCHEMY COULD *MAKE* HIS OWN *NOOSE*.

MAYBE IT'LL BE A NOOSE, DOCTOR ZOLOMON...

...BUT I'M THINKING IT MIGHT BE *MORE* LIKE A *LEASH*...

...AND THAT *THIS* IS JUST ONE *WILD-GOOSE CHASE*.

ALPHA HOLDING

SIR? YOU HAVE A *MINUTE?*

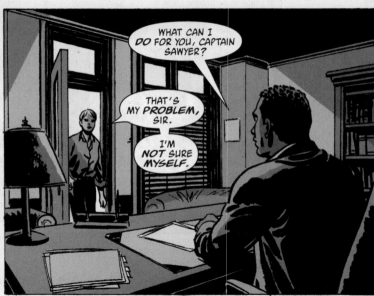

WHAT CAN I *DO* FOR YOU, CAPTAIN SAWYER?

THAT'S MY *PROBLEM,* SIR.

I'M *NOT* SURE MYSELF.

ALL RIGHT, I'M *INTRIGUED.*

EXPLAIN, MAGGIE.

IT'S ABOUT THE *THING* WITH OFFICER KELLY.

ALLEN AND MONTOYA ARE OUT IN *KEYSTONE,* THEY'VE BEEN TALKING TO DOCTOR ALCHEMY. THEY WANT TO *BRING* HIM *HERE.*

ALCHEMY HAS ADMITTED THAT HE'S *RESPONSIBLE* FOR KELLY'S CONDITION?

YES, SIR, COMMISSIONER.

THING IS, ALCHEMY'S *ALSO* CLAIMING HE CAN *CURE* KELLY.

BUT HE NEEDS TO *SEE* THE...*PATIENT*... FIRST.

OF COURSE HE DOES.

126

MONTOYA AND ALLEN, THEY THINK HE'S ON THE *LEVEL*?

IF THERE IS A *CURE*, ALCHEMY KNOWS IT.

WHETHER HE'LL *DO* IT OR *NOT*, THAT'S SOMETHING *ELSE*.

YOU'VE SPOKEN TO THE KEYSTONE PEOPLE ABOUT TRANSFERRING DOCTOR ALCHEMY TO OUR *CUSTODY*?

I MADE SOME INITIAL *INQUIRIES*, BUT ULTIMATELY, IT HAS TO COME FROM *YOU* AND THE DISTRICT ATTORNEY.

WOULD WE BE TRYING THIS *HARD* TO SAVE KELLY IF HE *WASN'T* A COP, MAGGIE?

I DON'T KNOW.

BUT HE *IS* A COP, MIKE...

...AND ACCORDING TO *EVERYONE* WHO KNOWS HIM, A DAMN *GOOD* ONE.

AND THERE ARE *FEW* ENOUGH OF *THOSE* IN THIS CITY.

ALL RIGHT, I'LL CALL THEIR D.A.

THANK YOU, SIR.

...SO IT'S **APPROVED**, THEN?

NOK NOK NOK

...WHAT DO YOU MEAN, A **CONDITION**? WHAT DOES THAT MEAN, **MORILLO**?

...AND YOU GUYS **CLEARED** THAT WITH **OUR** PEOPLE ALREADY...?

...HUH...NO, DOESN'T **BUG** ME, WE'VE GOT **ENOUGH** FREAKS IN GOTHAM, WE DON'T NEED TO ADD **YOURS**, TOO...

...HEH, NO, THAT'S A **DIFFERENT** STORY...

ALL RIGHT, WE'LL SEE YOU AT THE **AIRPORT**.

Carmine's Pizza
BEST IN SILVER

DONE DEAL?

YEAH. MORILLO AND CHYRE WILL **ESCORT** ALCHEMY TO GOTHAM **WITH** US ON THE **RED-EYE** TONIGHT, TAKE HIM **BACK** AS SOON AS WE'RE **DONE**.

THAT WAY, KEYSTONE **MAINTAINS** CUSTODY, AS OPPOSED TO RENDERING HIM TO US.

GOOD FOR **US**, ROTTEN FOR **THEM**, ESPECIALLY IF **SOMETHING** HAPPENS.

TELL ME ABOUT IT.

HOLD ON...

...**DAMMIT**...

DEE? HEY, IT'S **ME**. GUESS YOU'RE STILL AT THE **RESTAURANT**...

...CRIS AND I ARE STILL IN **KEYSTONE**, WE'RE FLYING BACK LATE TONIGHT.

JUST WANTED TO SAY THAT I MISS YOU...

...AND I LOVE YOU.

≈KLIK≈

I BEG YOUR *PARDON*...

...I'M LOOKING FOR MY *DAUGHTER,* RENEE...

...I UNDERSTAND SHE LIVES...HERE...

...YOU...YOU MUST BE MS. HERNANDEZ?

DARIA HERNANDEZ.

RENEE'S *NOT* HERE RIGHT NOW, SHE'S OUT OF *TOWN*--

I SEE.

I...I WON'T *TROUBLE* YOU, THEN...

MISTER MONTOYA.

PERHAPS...

WOULD YOU LIKE TO COME INSIDE?

PERHAPS FOR A FEW MINUTES, THANK YOU.

YOU DON'T WANT TO PICK UP ANYTHING FOR DORE? OR YOUR KIDS?

MY *WIFE* AND *KIDS* DON'T NEED A *SHIRT* PROVING THAT I *SURVIVED* A *FLIGHT* TO KEYSTONE CITY.

THIS HASN'T BEEN A *TOURIST* TRIP, PARTNER.

YOU'RE *AFRAID* TO FLY. THAT'S *IT*, ISN'T IT?

SHUT UP.

HERE THEY *ARE*.

NOTHING *QUITE* AS DEPRESSING AS AN *AIRPORT* IN THE MIDDLE OF THE *NIGHT*, IS THERE?

THE *REEK* OF *MELANCHOLY* AND *DESPERATION*.

DETECTIVE *DYKE* AND DETECTIVE *STOWE*. HOW *NICE* TO *SEE* YOU BOTH AGAIN.

STOWE?

HARRIET BEECHER STOWE. WROTE *UNCLE TOM'S CABIN*.

SEE, HE'S CALLING ME AN UNCLE TOM.

REALLY, DETECTIVE *CHYRE*, IF YOU NEED THESE THINGS *EXPLAINED* TO YOU, YOU'RE NOT GOING TO GET VERY *FAR* IN YOUR *CHOSEN* PROFESSION.

LUCKILY, WE HAVE THE *ENTIRE* FLIGHT TO WORK ON YOUR *CONTINUING* EDUCATION.

FIRST PUBLISHED IN 1852, *UNCLE TOM'S CABIN, OR LIFE AMONG THE LOWLY*, IS CONSIDERED BY *MANY* TO BE ONE OF THE *CAUSES* THAT LED TO THE CIVIL WAR...

DOCTOR LING, DOCTOR LING TO THE O.R.

DOCTOR VILLEGAS, PLEASE DIAL EXTENSION 5530.

...HEY...

HEY!

HELLO?

IS SOMEONE HERE?

ANDY? GOD,
ANDY, CAN YOU
HEAR ME?

SHHHAARONNN?

THE
KID...

...DID
KID...GET
OUUUTT...?

HE'S FINE, ANDY,
YOU *SAVED* HIM. HE'S
FINE, THEY'RE
BOTH FINE.

OH, GOD,
ANDY...

NOOO...

...DOONNN'T
CRY...

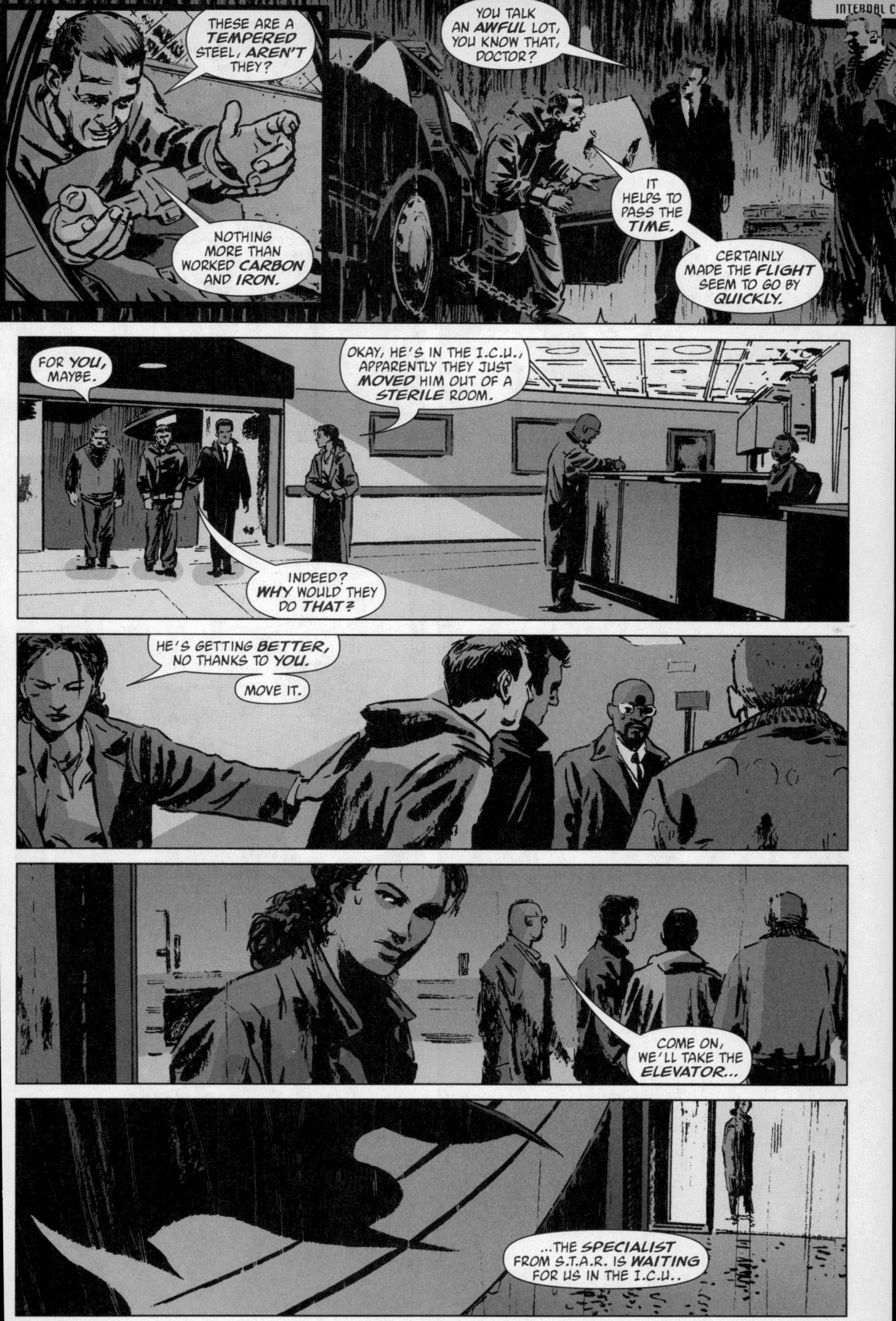
THESE ARE A TEMPERED STEEL, AREN'T THEY?
NOTHING MORE THAN WORKED CARBON AND IRON.
YOU TALK AN AWFUL LOT, YOU KNOW THAT, DOCTOR?
IT HELPS TO PASS THE TIME.
CERTAINLY MADE THE FLIGHT SEEM TO GO BY QUICKLY.
FOR YOU, MAYBE.
OKAY, HE'S IN THE I.C.U., APPARENTLY THEY JUST MOVED HIM OUT OF A STERILE ROOM.
INDEED? WHY WOULD THEY DO THAT?
HE'S GETTING BETTER, NO THANKS TO YOU.
MOVE IT.
COME ON, WE'LL TAKE THE ELEVATOR...
...THE SPECIALIST FROM S.T.A.R. IS WAITING FOR US IN THE I.C.U..

THAT WAS ROUGHLY *ONE* THIS MORNING.

HE'S BEEN *DRIFTING* IN AND OUT OF CONSCIOUSNESS EVER SINCE, BUT FOR THE TIME BEING, I'D SAY THAT OFFICER KELLY IS *STABLE.*

THEN YOU'RE AN *IDIOT.*

I BEG YOUR *PARDON?*

MONKEY WANT A 'NANA?

YOU'RE AN *IDIOT,* AN *IMBECILE,* A *MORON.*

WHAT DO YOU HAVE HIM ON? STEROIDS?

IT SEEMED THE *BEST* WAY TO *BOLSTER*--

YEAH, *IDIOT,* IT'S *NOT* HELPING HIM, IT'S *MASKING* THE *SYMPTOMS,* ALL RIGHT?

AND WHEN HE *DECOMPENSATES*-- AND HE *WILL,* SWEET CHEEKS--HE'LL *DIE,* DO YOU UNDER- STAND?

I'LL USE *SMALL* WORDS:

YOU. ARE. KILLING. HIM.

YOU'RE THE *LUNATIC* WHO *DID* THIS TO HIM?

GUILTY AS CHARGED.

THEN WHY IN THE *WORLD* WOULD I BELIEVE YOU CARE ABOUT *CURING* HIM?

MY *EXPERIMENT* WAS TO *CHANGE* HIM, *NOT* MURDER HIM.

AND YOU, YOU'RE *MURDERING* HIM, *NOT CURING* HIM.

LOOK, WE **BROUGHT** HIM ALL THIS **WAY** TO TAKE A **LOOK** AT HIM--

I'M **NOT** LETTING THIS **SOCIOPATH** NEAR MY **PATIENT**--

SCIENTIST! I'M A **SCIENTIST**--

EEE

--YOU BUBBLE-CHESTED **BIMBO** IN A LAB **COAT!**

EEEEE

EEEEESEEEEEEEEEEE

NURSE!

PADDLES!

OH NO, NO, NO--

HE'S **READY.**

--GOD NO PLEASE **PLEASE** NO--

AS AM I.

YOU KNOW THE *LEGEND* OF THE *PHILOSOPHER'S STONE,* DETECTIVES?

TRANSMUTING LEAD INTO *GOLD?*

CARBON AND *IRON* INTO HYDROGEN AND OXYGEN?

OR PERHAPS THE *STERLING SILVER* OF A SPECIAL *NECKLACE--*

SON OF A--

--INTO *HYDROGEN* AND *CHLORINE?*

¿GHFF¿

HKHKKRRRRK

136

DROP--

HKKRKK

SSHHHHSSSSS

--IIITTTTTT

MY THOUGHT PRECISELY.

OFFICER KELLY...

...THE DOCTOR WILL SEE YOU NOW.

HNHAAARRHh

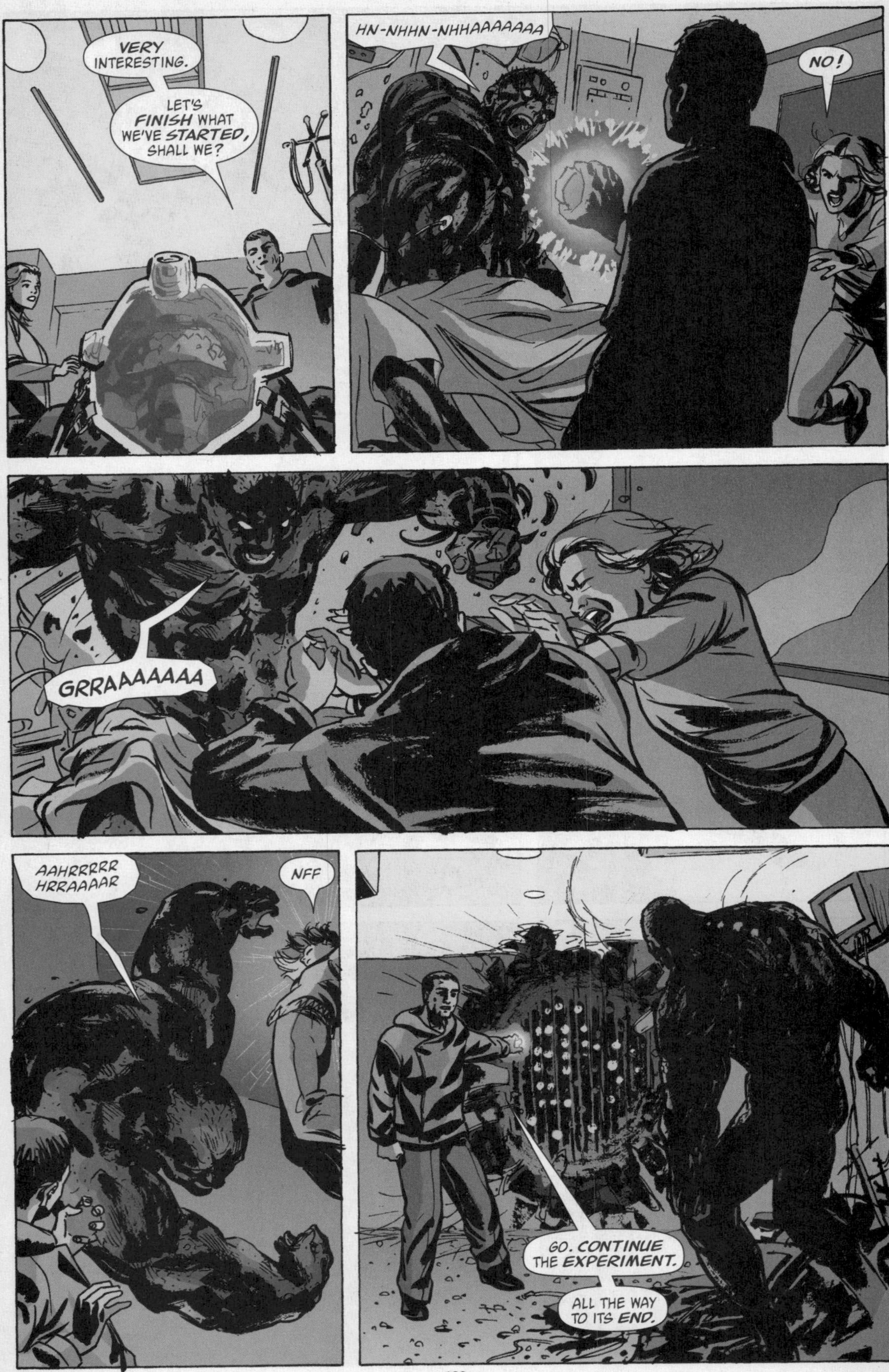
VERY INTERESTING.
LET'S FINISH WHAT WE'VE STARTED, SHALL WE?
HN-NHHN-NHHAAAAAAA
NO!
GRRAAAAAAA
AAHRRRRR HRRAAAAR
NFF
GO. CONTINUE THE EXPERIMENT.
ALL THE WAY TO ITS END.

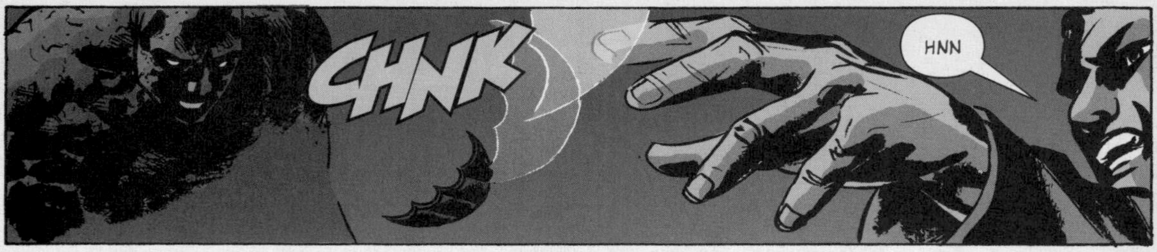
CHNK
HNN

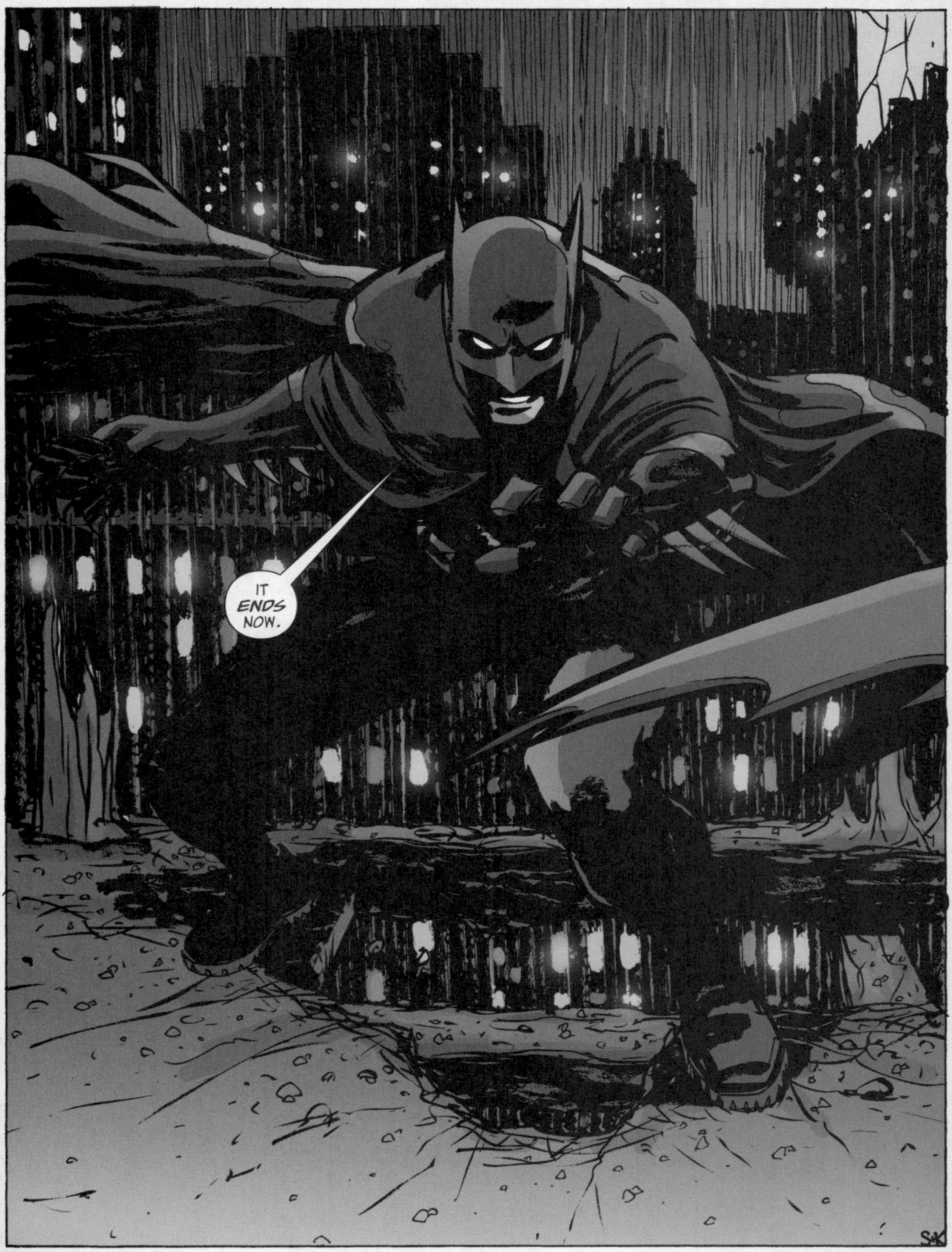
IT ENDS NOW.

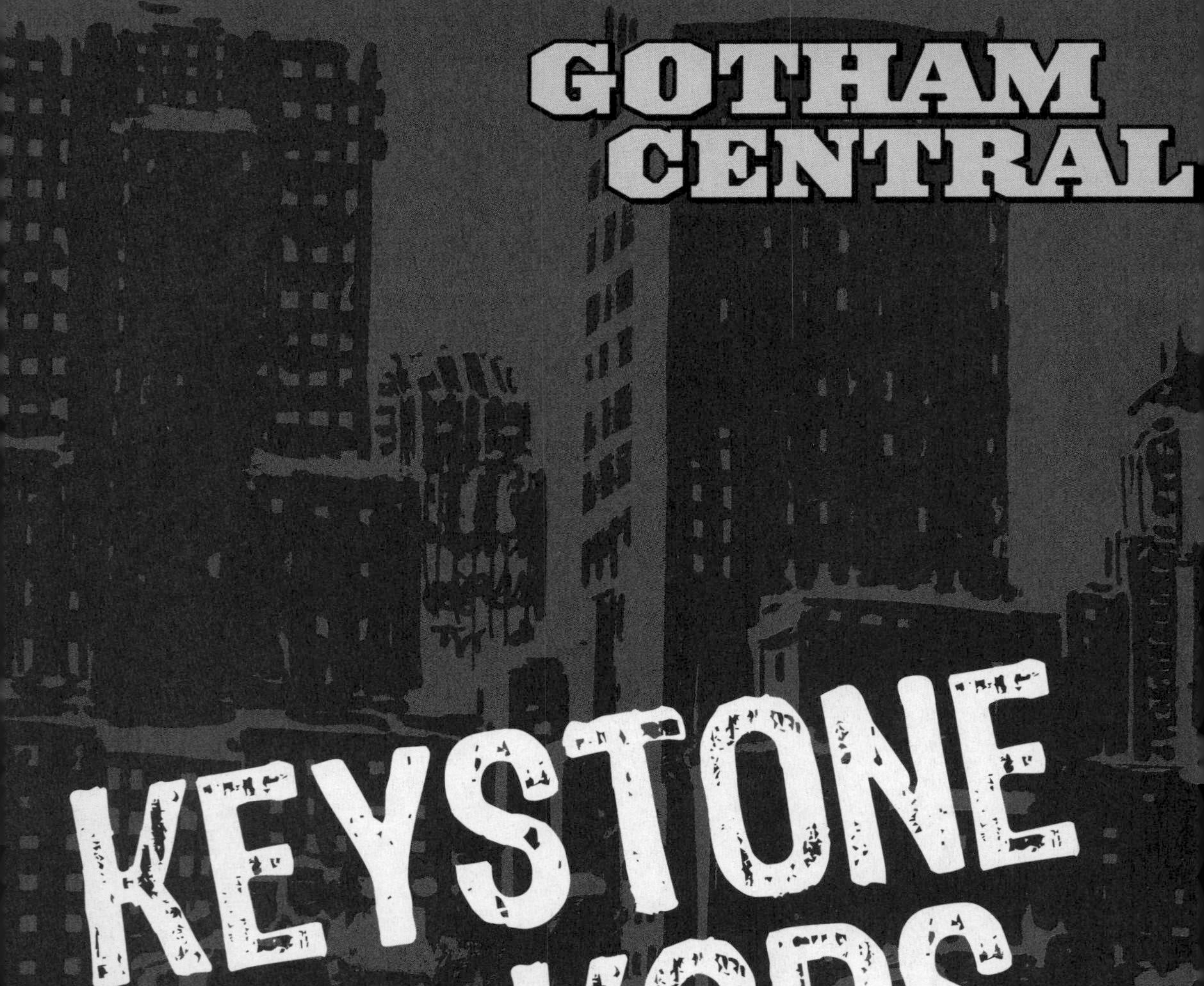

GOTHAM CENTRAL

KEYSTONE KOPS

PART FOUR

GREG RUCKA
WRITER

STEFANO GAUDIANO
PENCILLER

GARY AMARO
INKER

--WARNED THEM ABOUT *YOU*, ALCHEMY, BUT THEY *DIDN'T* LISTEN.

¿KAF KOFF?

THEY *NEVER* DO.

THE *PRICE* OF THE *SUPERIOR* INTELLECT, BATMAN...

SOME-THING YOU AND I *SHARE*, I BELIEVE.

WE SHARE *NOTHING.*

DON'T *MOVE,* DESMOND.

OH, DON'T *WORRY*, BATMAN, MY WORK HERE IS *DONE...*

141

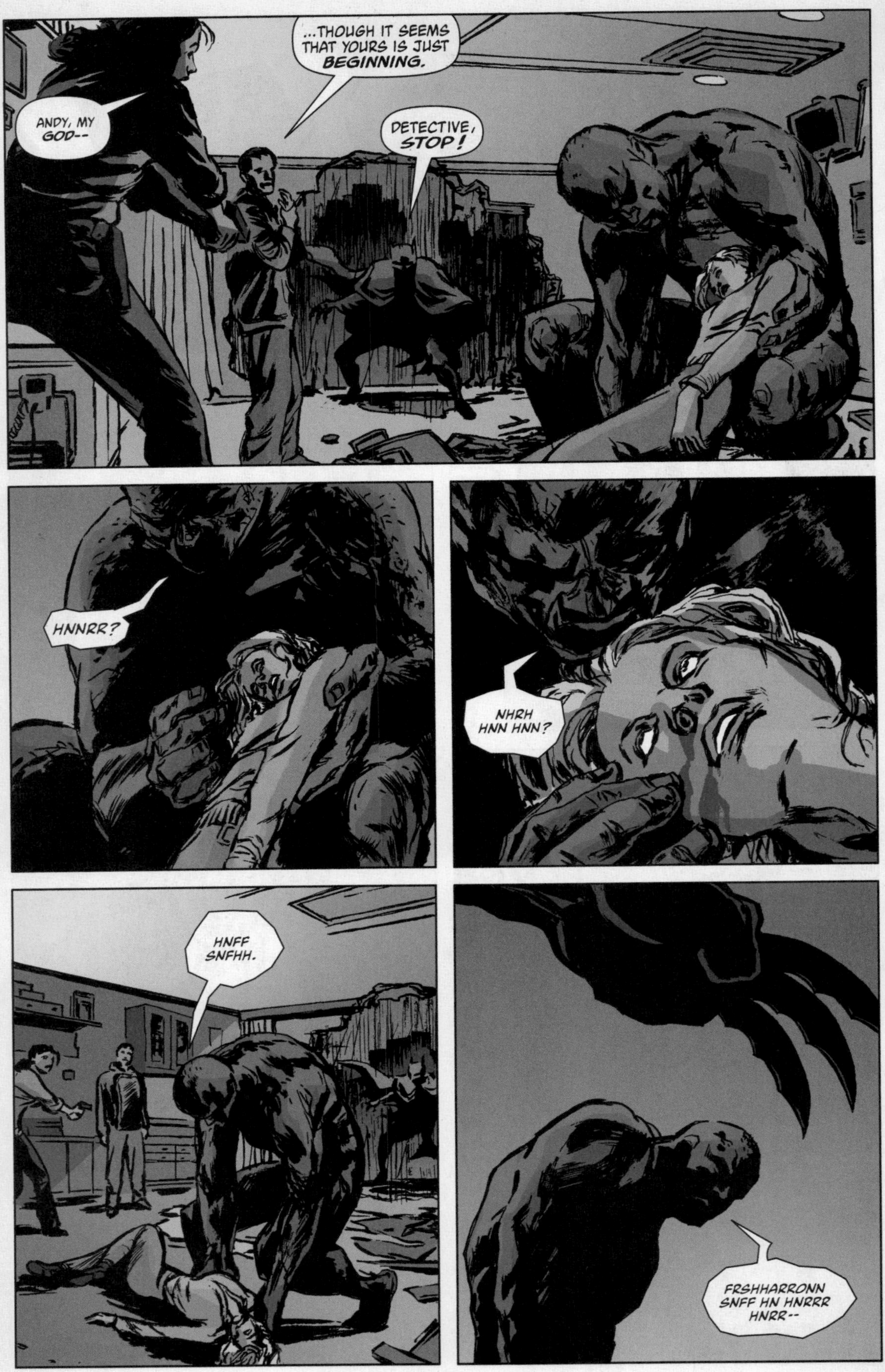
...THOUGH IT SEEMS THAT YOURS IS JUST BEGINNING.
ANDY, MY GOD--
DETECTIVE, STOP!
HNNRR?
NHRH HNN HNN?
HNFF SNFHH.
FRSHHARRONN SNFF HN HNRRR HNRR--

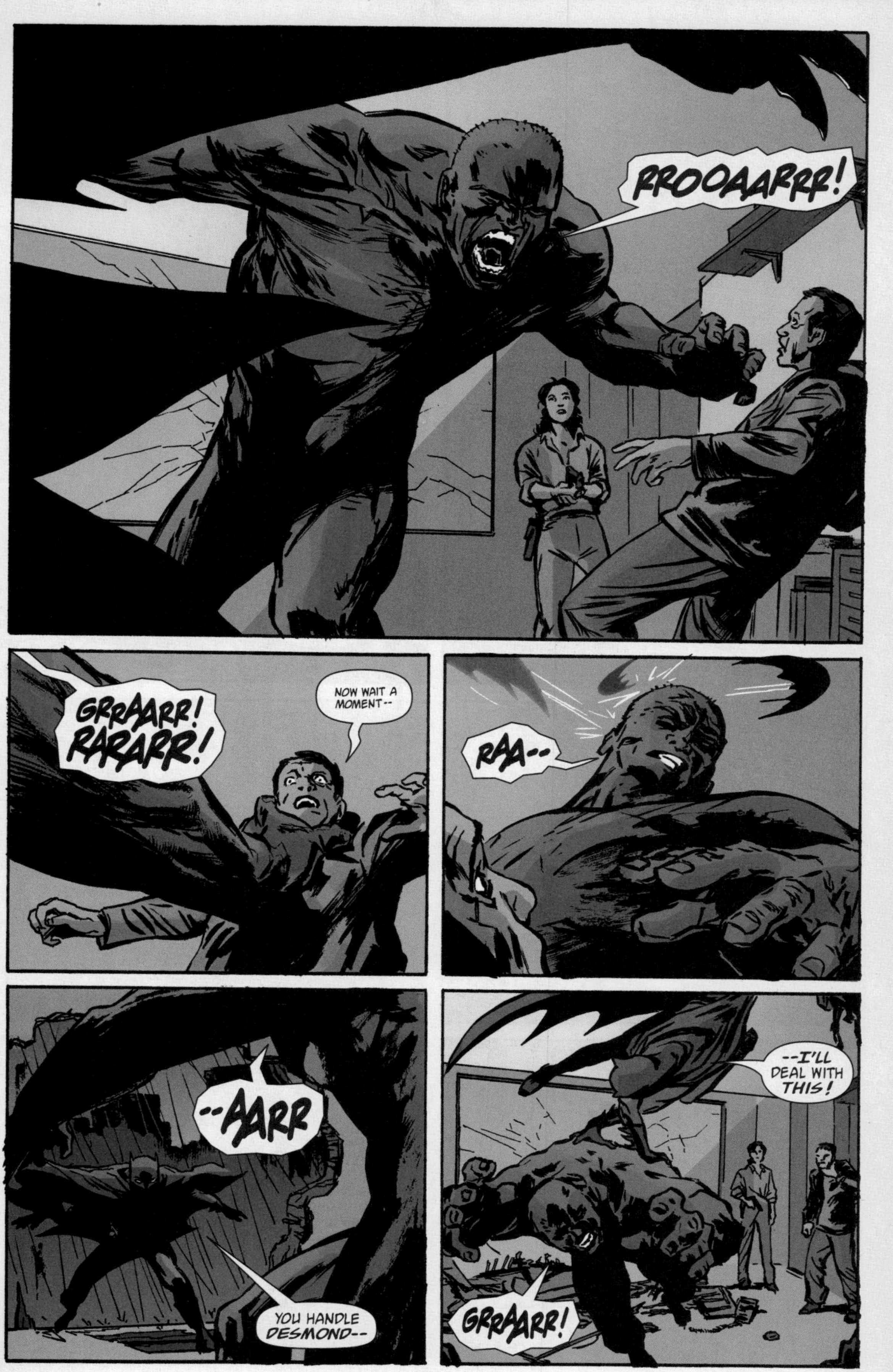
RROOAARRR!
GRRAARR! RARARR!
NOW WAIT A MOMENT--
RAA--
--AARR
YOU HANDLE DESMOND--
--I'LL DEAL WITH THIS!
GRRAARR!

ARRAARRRRR

YOU'RE IN THE **WRONG** TOWN, DOC.

I'VE **NEVER** HIT MY **GIRL**--

GHUH

--BUT I'LL **SURE** AS HELL BEAT **YOUR** ASS, MOTHER$#%*!

HKKK

144

...ALL UNITS, BUT THERE'S BEEN *NOTHING* FOR OVER AN *HOUR*.

SUN'S COMING *UP*, SO IT SHOULD MAKE THE *HUNT* EASIER.

NO CHANCE BATMAN CAUGHT UP WITH HIM?

IF HE *HAD*, WE'D HAVE *HEARD* ABOUT IT BY NOW.

YOU USE THAT *SIGNAL* THING OF YOURS?

NOT ANYMORE, WE DON'T.

MUST *SUCK* NOT TO BE ABLE TO *TRUST* YOUR GUY.

TELL ME ABOUT IT.

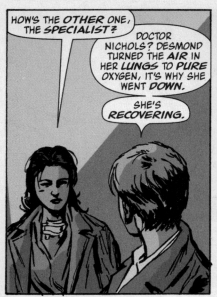

HOW'S THE *OTHER* ONE, THE *SPECIALIST?*

DOCTOR *NICHOLS?* DESMOND TURNED THE *AIR* IN HER *LUNGS* TO *PURE OXYGEN,* IT'S WHY SHE WENT *DOWN.*

SHE'S *RECOVERING.*

WHAT NOW, CAP?

UNTIL WE *FIND* KELLY, NOT A LOT WE *CAN* DO.

YOU TWO SHOULD GET OUT OF *HERE,* GET CLEANED UP, GET SOME *REST...*

...I'LL CALL IF ANYTHING *DEVELOPS.*

WELL, MORILLO, WE'RE GONNA HAVE TO *HOLD* ONTO *DESMOND* FOR A FEW DAYS, AT LEAST TO *CHARGE* HIM.

WHAT ABOUT US, CAPTAIN SAWYER?

YOU MEAN *AFTER* HE GETS OUT OF THE *E.R.*

LOOK, WE'RE *HERE,* CAPTAIN, WE'RE WILLING TO *HELP...*

HEY, MONTOYA...

YEAH, CHYRE?

THAT *MAKEOVER* YOU GAVE DOCTOR ALCHEMY.

YEAH?

NICELY DONE.

:KAFF:
:KOFF:

:KOFF:
:KAFF:

HEY.

HOW LONG YOU BEEN BACK?

NOT LONG.

:KAFF:

DIDN'T WANT TO WAKE YOU, SORRY--

OH MY GOD, RENEE--

--WHAT HAPPENED, DID YOU GET BURNED?

WHAT?

YOUR SKIN...

...LOOKS LIKE YOU GOT BURNED...

DOCTOR ALCHEMY SOUNDS POSITIVELY *VILE*.

YEAH, WELL, THAT'S WHY THEY CALL PEOPLE LIKE DESMOND *SUPERVILLAINS*, DEE.

AND YOU'RE *OKAY?* YOU FEEL ALL RIGHT?

THE *COUGH* FINALLY SEEMS TO HAVE GONE AWAY.

I'M JUST *TIRED*.

I'LL HAVE TO GET YOU A *NEW* NECKLACE.

DON'T YOU THINK IT'LL BE KIND OF *REDUNDANT?*

RENEE.

I'M JUST SAYING.

YOUR *FATHER* STOPPED BY WHILE YOU WERE IN KEYSTONE.

WHAT'D HE WANT?

TO SEE YOU.

HE *MISSES* YOU, RENEE...

...HE WANTS YOU *BACK* IN HIS LIFE.

MORNING, HERNANDO!

MORNING, VICTOR!

HAVE A GOOD DAY!

YOU, TOO.

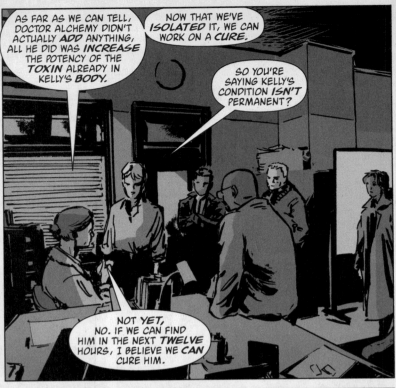

...COMPARED KELLY'S BLOOD BEFORE **AND** AFTER ALCHEMY **ZAPPED** HIM.

AS FAR AS WE CAN TELL, DOCTOR ALCHEMY DIDN'T ACTUALLY **ADD** ANYTHING, ALL HE DID WAS **INCREASE** THE POTENCY OF THE **TOXIN** ALREADY IN KELLY'S **BODY.**

NOW THAT WE'VE **ISOLATED** IT, WE CAN WORK ON A **CURE.**

SO YOU'RE SAYING KELLY'S CONDITION **ISN'T** PERMANENT?

NOT **YET,** NO. IF WE CAN FIND HIM IN THE NEXT **TWELVE** HOURS, I BELIEVE WE **CAN** CURE HIM.

WE'RE TALKING ABOUT KELLY?

DOCTOR NICHOLS THINKS THERE'S A WAY TO CHANGE HIM BACK--

⸢KAFF KOFFKOFF⸥

WHAT DO YOU **NEED** FROM US?

PARDON ME.

YOU NEED TO **FIND** KELLY, **SUBDUE** HIM SOMEHOW.

THE **SOONER** I CAN ATTEND TO HIM, THE **BETTER** HIS CHANCES **ARE.**

WE HAVE **ANY** IDEA WHERE HE **IS?**

NOTHING AT ALL.

DESMOND **MIGHT** KNOW.

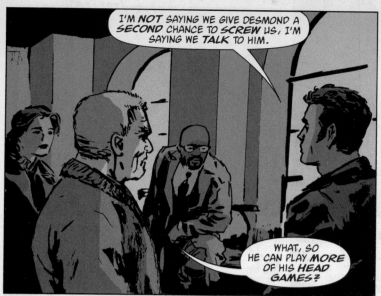

I'M **NOT** SAYING WE GIVE DESMOND A **SECOND** CHANCE TO **SCREW** US, I'M SAYING WE **TALK** TO HIM.

WHAT, SO HE CAN PLAY **MORE** OF HIS **HEAD** GAMES?

YOU GOT A **BETTER** IDEA, I'M **LISTENING**, FRED.

DESMOND STILL AT THE **HOSPITAL**?

HE WAS MOVED TO THE **SCHRECK** THREE HOURS AGO, UNDER **MAXIMUM** SECURITY.

WE'LL KEEP YOU **POSTED**, CAPTAIN.

¿KOFF KOFF KOFF KOFF?

YOU DO THAT.

DING DING

OFFICER PEAK? I DIDN'T **RECOGNIZE** YOU OUT OF YOUR **UNIFORM.**

HEY, HERNANDO.

YEAH, I'M, UH... I'M TAKING THE **DAY...**

...OFF...

YOU DON'T LOOK SO GOOD, OFFICER.

ANDY'S ON THE **LOOSE,** I DON'T KNOW IF YOU **HEARD** IT ON THE **NEWS.**

TURNED INTO A **MONSTER** OR SOMETHING, HE'S...

...HE...HE **KILLED** HIS **GIRLFRIEND,** SHARON, HERNANDO...

...AT THE **HOSPITAL,** HE WAS OUT OF **CONTROL** AND HE...HE...

...I KEPT **TELLING** HER IT WOULD BE **OKAY...**

...I TOLD HER EVERYTHING WOULD BE **OKAY...**

YOU'LL GET NO HELP FROM ME.

IN FACT, THE ONLY THING YOU'LL BE GETTING FROM ME IS A MASSIVE SUIT FOR DAMAGES, FILED AGAINST DETECTIVE DYKE FOR BRUTALITY.

YOU WERE RESISTING ARREST.

SPTT

DAMNIT--

RENEE!

--GET OFF OF ME!

UH-OH, LOOK OUT--

--ANGRY LESBIAN, COMING THROUGH!

I'LL BE OUTSIDE.

NO, DON'T LEAVE...

...YOUR BUTTONS ARE SO EASY TO PRESS!

I MEAN IT, DETECTIVE! YOUR SUBCONSCIOUS IS SO CLOSE TO THE SURFACE I CAN SEE ITS PERISCOPE!

SHUT UP, ALBERT.

...DOWN TO THE *BUS* TO TAKE 'EM ALL TO *COURT* FOR THE *TEN* A.M...

--MONSTER, I'M TELLING YOU HE'S [LI]KE A GREEN HULKING MONSTER--

--DIDN'T *DO* ANYTHING I *SWEAR* TO *GOD!!!*

...FOLLOW THE [R]ED LINE *PAINTED* ON THE FLOOR, TURN *LEFT...*

--JUST WANTED HIM TO PAY *ME* WHAT HE *OWED*--

--I DON'T *DO* FREEBIES, *THAT'S* WHY I *CUT* HIM--

HEY, MONTOYA!

OFFICER DOGNAVICH.

HEARD YOU GOT THE S.O.B. WHO *DID* KELLY.

HEARD YOU *WORKED* HIM OVER PRETTY *GOOD.*

GOOD *JOB.*

WHAT'S *YOUR* PROBLEM?

HNNKIDDZZ

SSVVVTHHKIDDZZZ

SKRREE

HNKK
HNKK

155

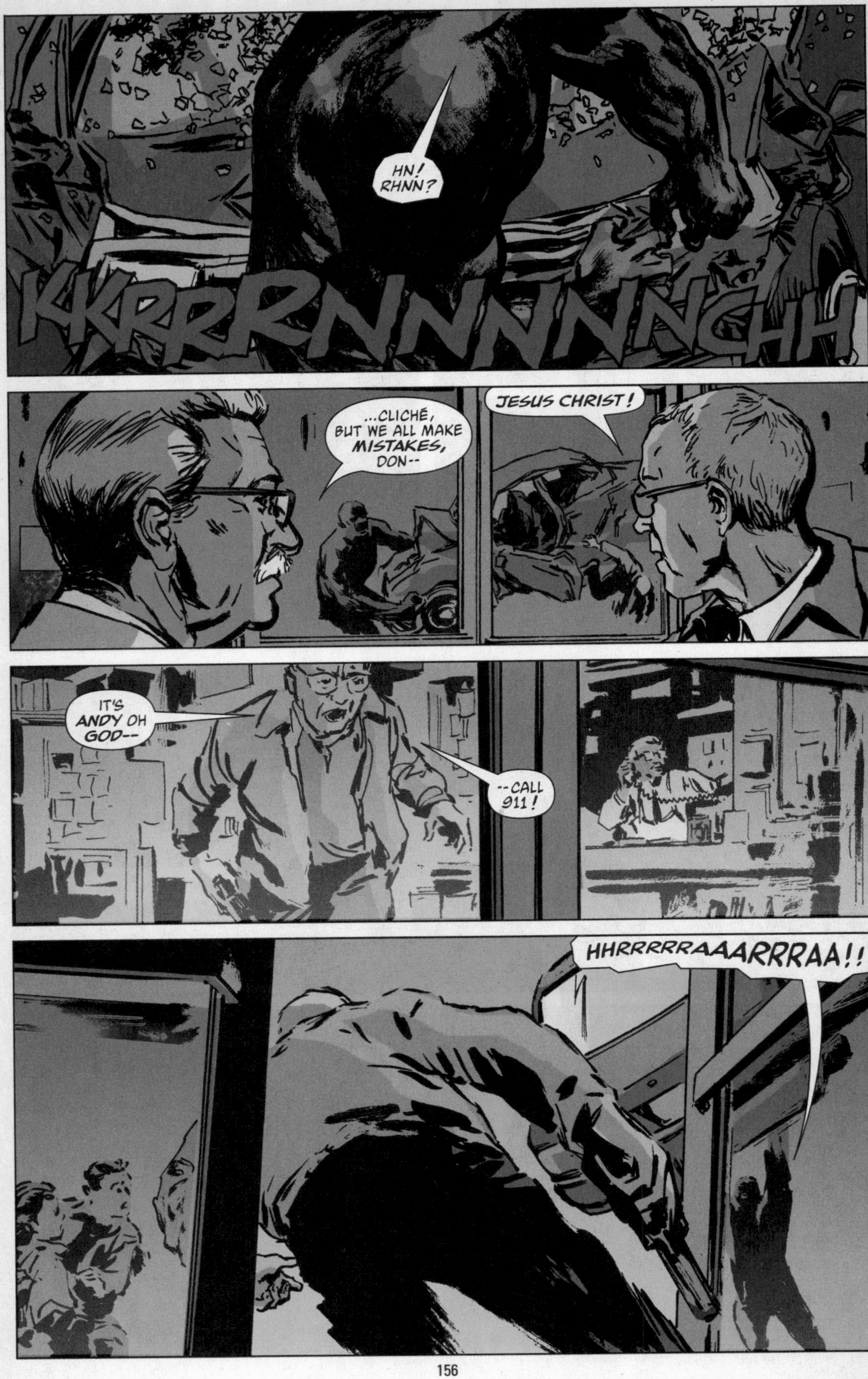
HN! RHNN?
KKRRRNNNNNCHH
...CLICHÉ, BUT WE ALL MAKE MISTAKES, DON--
JESUS CHRIST!
IT'S ANDY OH GOD--
--CALL 911!
HHRRRRRAAARRRAA!!

...RESOLVED, TEN-FIFTY. BACK IN SERVICE. {SKSS}

{SKCHH} ANGEL FOUR-ELEVEN, TEN-FOUR. {SKCHH}

{SKSS} ALL UNITS, TEN-THIRTY-THREE IN PROGRESS...

...META-HUMAN DISTURBANCE, FIRE AND E.M.S. EN ROUTE...

...KELLY...

...FIFTEEN HUNDRED BLOCK AT VAN BUREN...

OH MY GOD--

RENEE?

RENEE, *WAIT!* WHERE THE HELL--

--OH MY GOD, PAPI--

--ARE YOU *GOING...?*

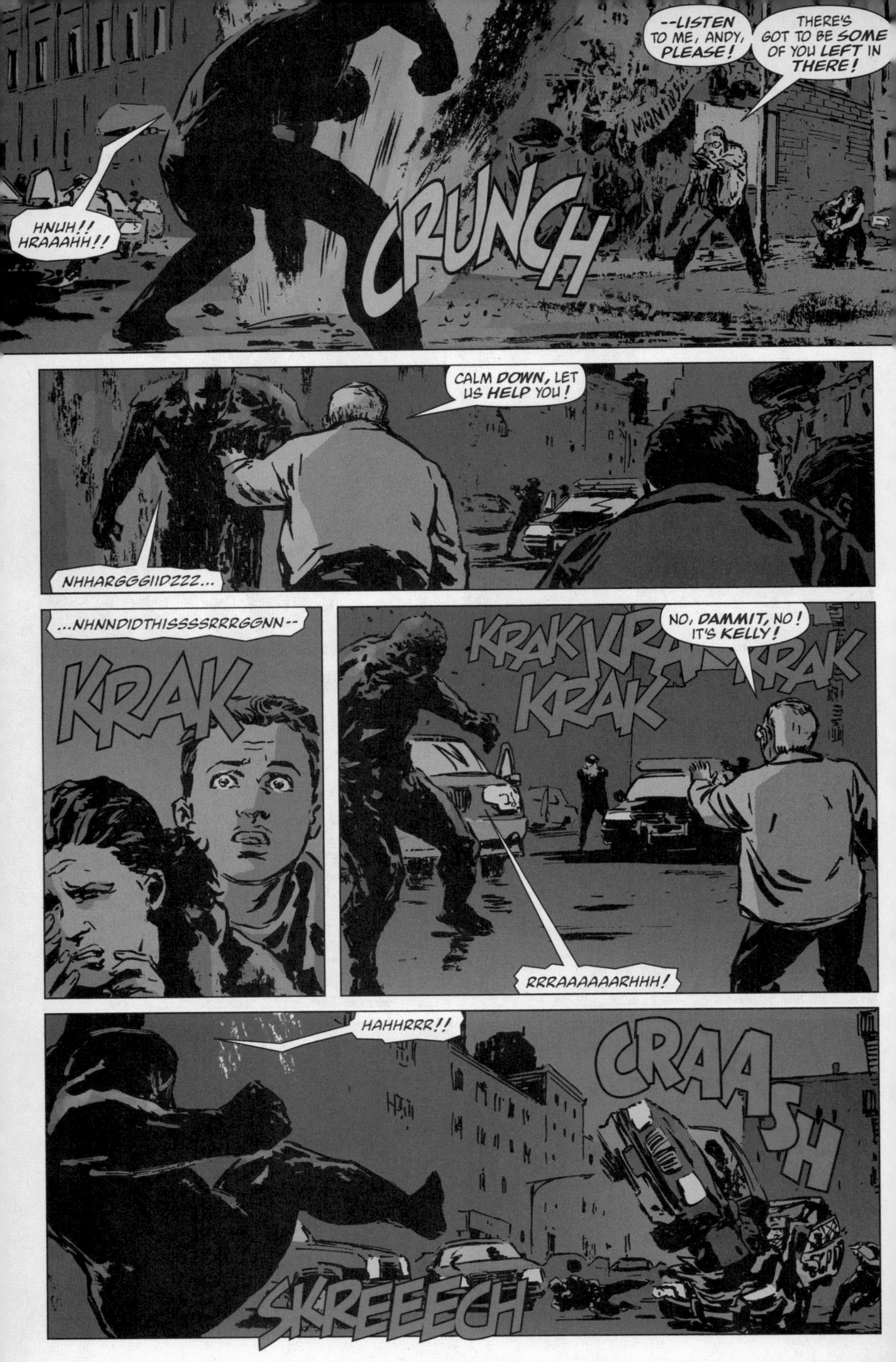
--LISTEN TO ME, ANDY, PLEASE!
THERE'S GOT TO BE SOME OF YOU LEFT IN THERE!
HNUH!! HRAAAHH!!
CRUNCH
CALM DOWN, LET US HELP YOU!
NHHARGGGIIDZZZ...
...NHNNDIDTHISSSSRRRGGNN--
KRAK
KRAK
KRAK
KRAK
KRAK
NO, DAMMIT, NO! IT'S KELLY!
RRRAAAAAAARHHH!
HAHHRRR!!
CRAASH
SKREEEECH

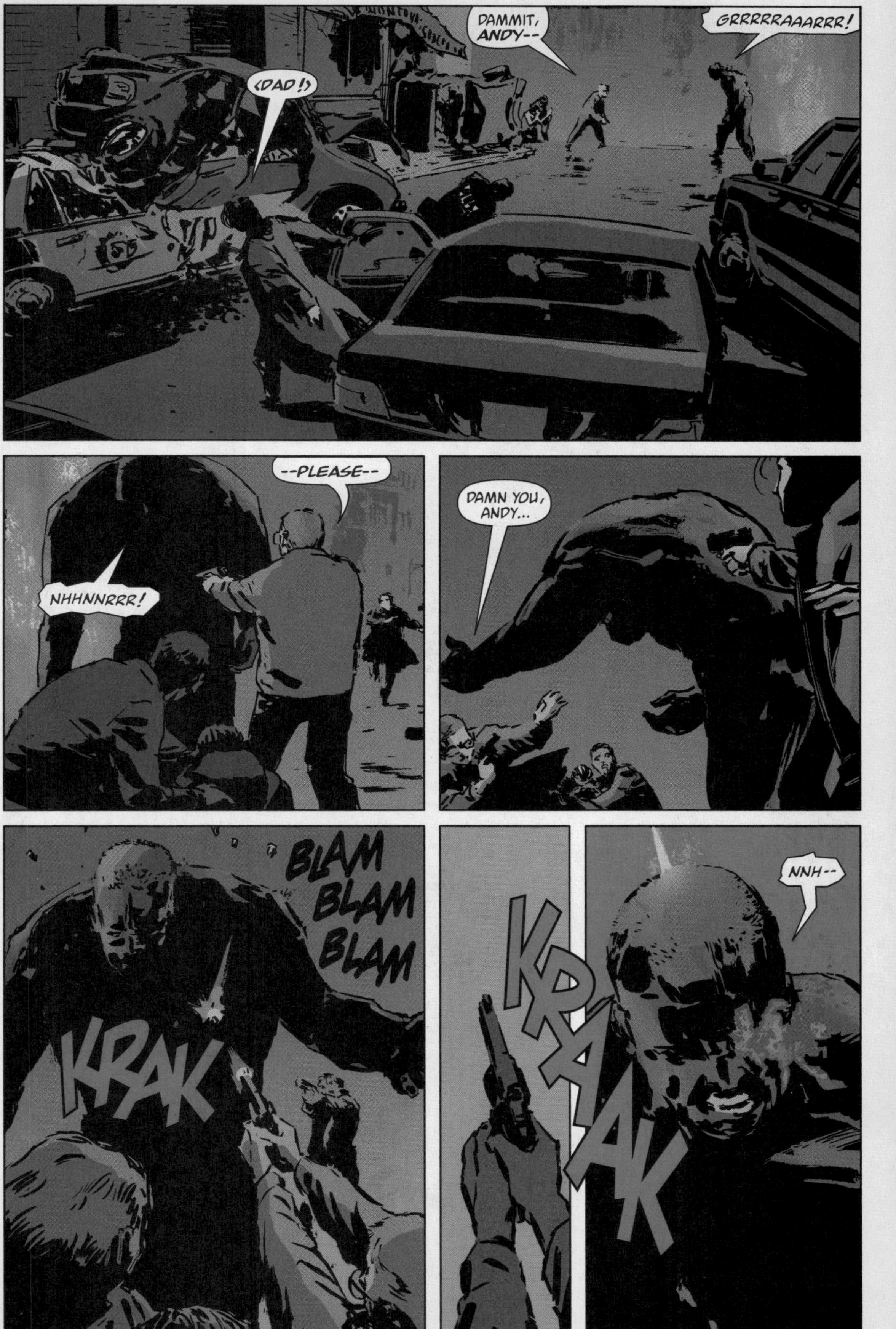
<DAD!>
DAMMIT, ANDY--
GRRRRRAAARRR!
--PLEASE--
NHHNNRRR!
DAMN YOU, ANDY...
BLAM BLAM BLAM
KRAK
KRAAK
NNH--

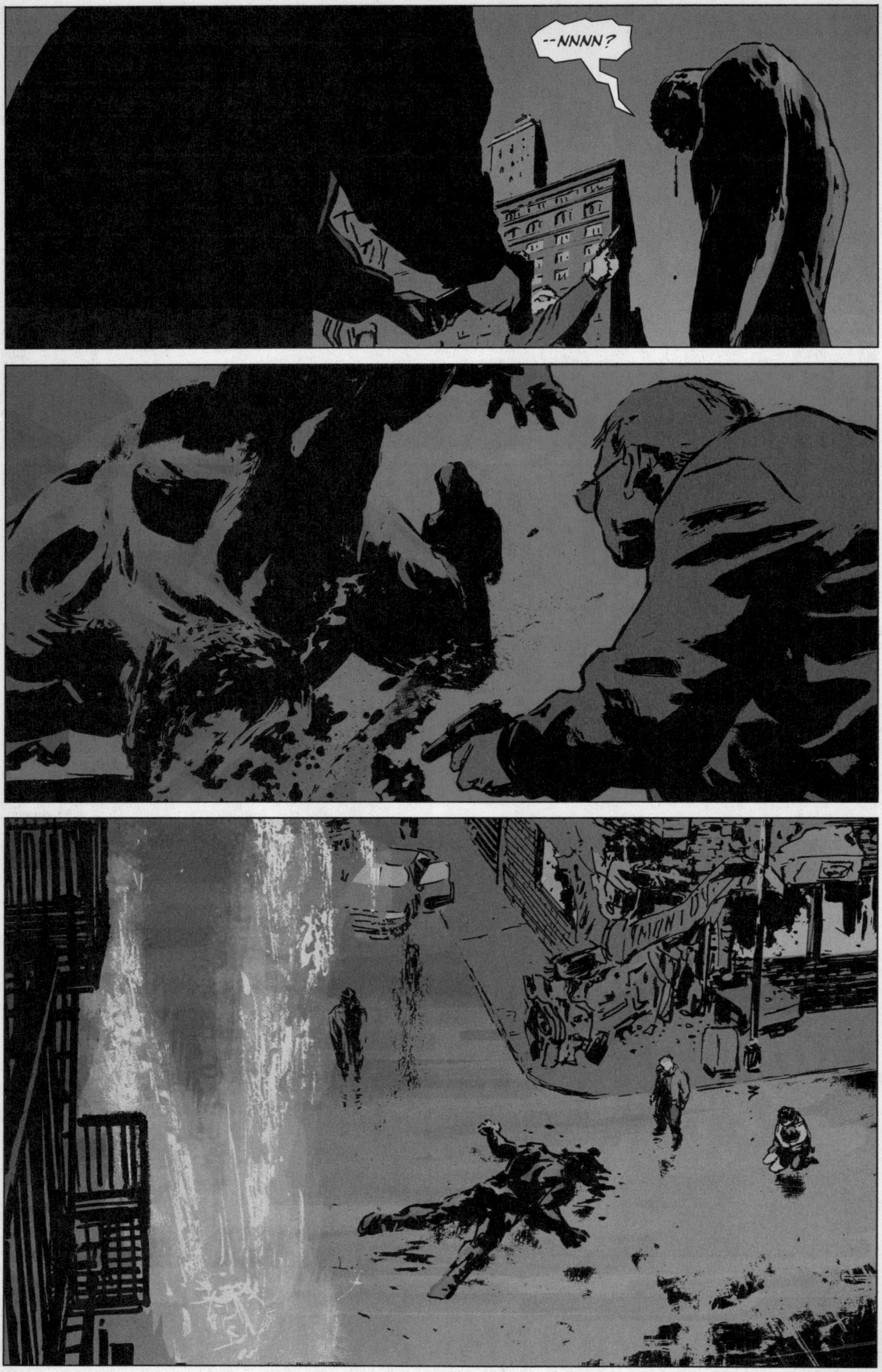
--NNNN?

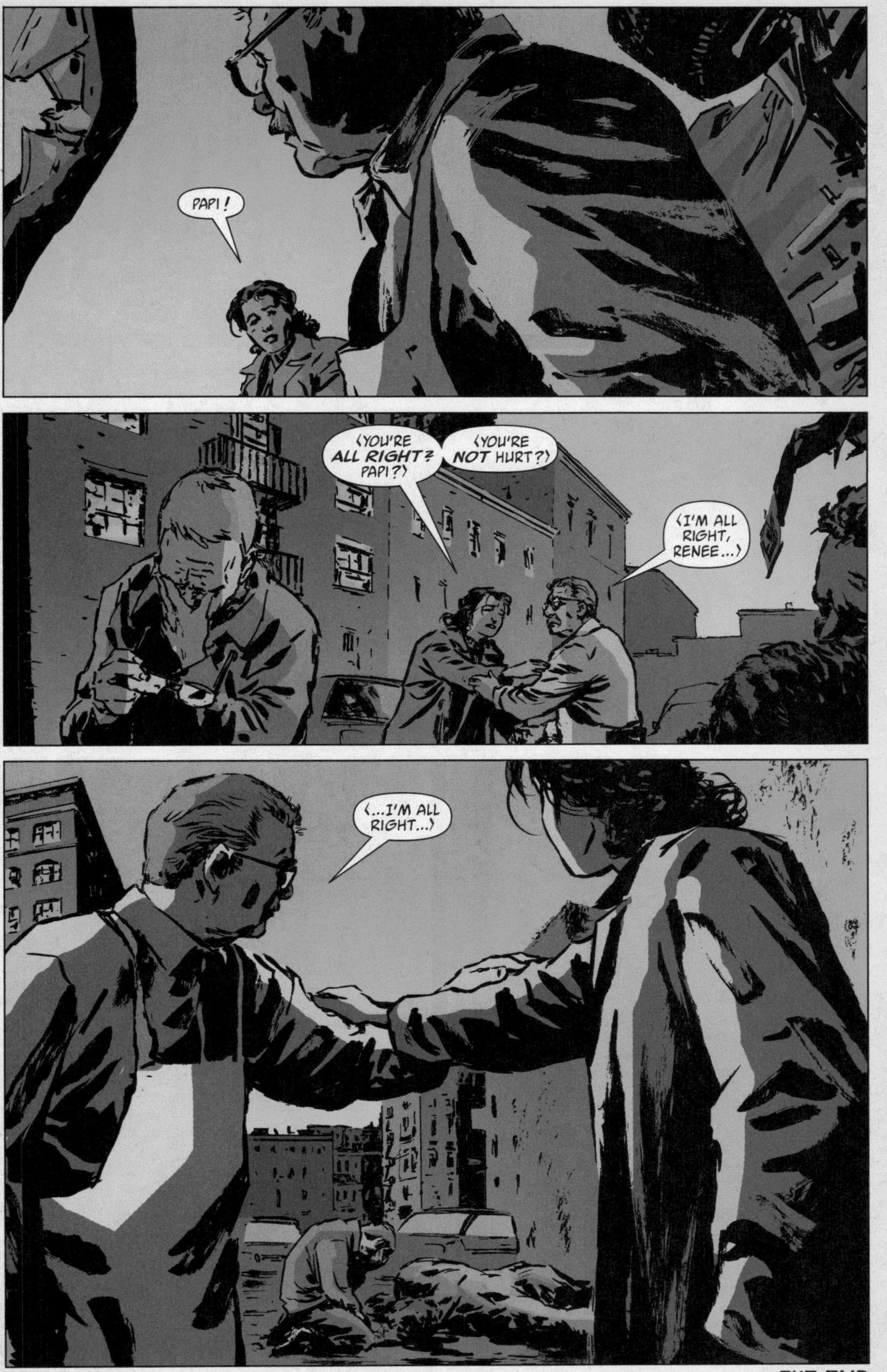
PAPI!
‹YOU'RE **ALL RIGHT?** PAPI?›
‹YOU'RE **NOT** HURT?›
‹I'M ALL RIGHT, RENEE...›
‹...I'M ALL RIGHT...›

THE END

GOTHAM CENTRAL #23 • ART BY MICHAEL LARK

GOTHAM CENTRAL #24 • ART BY MICHAEL LARK

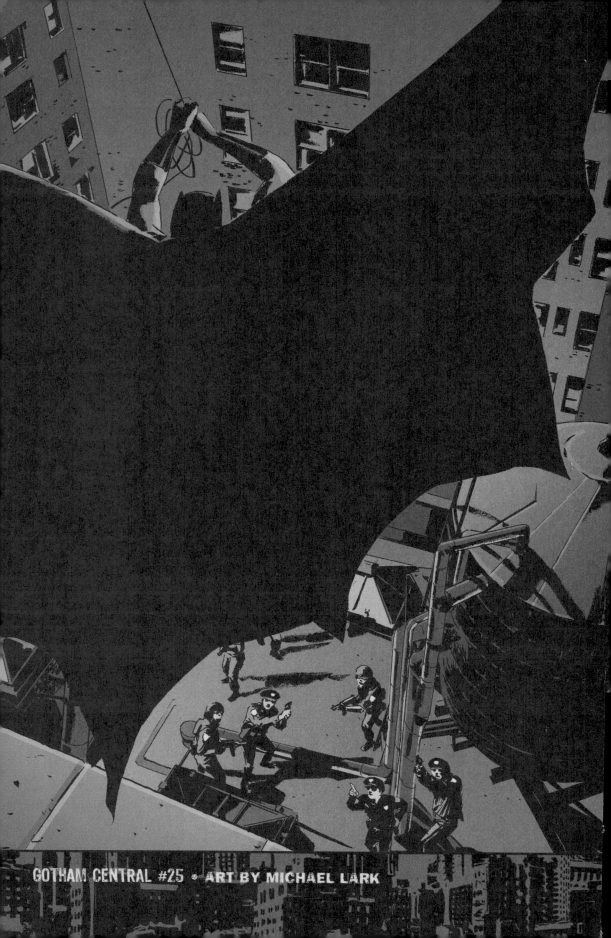

GOTHAM CENTRAL #25 · ART BY MICHAEL LARK

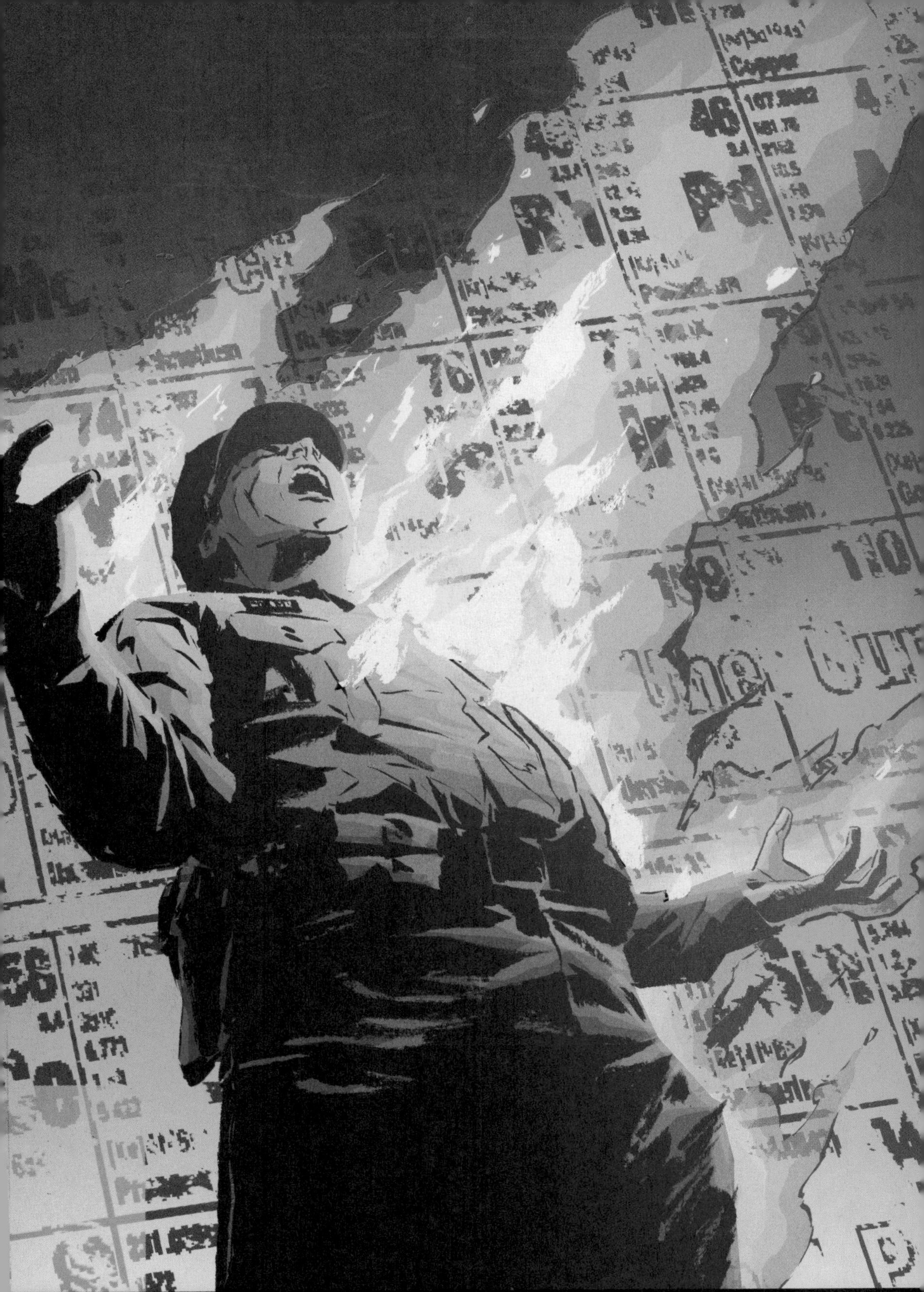

Copper
46
Pd
74
76
110

GOTHAM CENTRAL #29 · ART BY MICHAEL LARK

GOTHAM CENTRAL #30 • ART BY MICHAEL LARK

GOTHAM CENTRAL #31 • ART BY CLIFF CHIANG